THE MAKING OF MODERN LONDON 1815~1914

THE MAKING OF MODERN LONDON

1815~1914

**GAVIN WEIGHTMAN
STEVE HUMPHRIES**

Sidgwick & Jackson
London

First published in Great Britain
in 1983 by Sidgwick & Jackson
Limited

Reprinted November 1983

Designed by Ray Hyden

ISBN 0-283-99046-5 (soft cover)
ISBN 0-283-99050-3 (hard cover)

Printed in Great Britain by
Biddles Ltd, Guildford, Surrey
for Sidgwick & Jackson Limited
1 Tavistock Chambers
Bloomsbury Way
London WC1A 2SG

Previous pages: 'The Heart of the
Empire' by Niels M. Lund, painted in
1901.

To Jim and Marjorie Humphries, and Joyce

CONTENTS

Acknowledgments

We should like to thank all the people who have in one way or another helped us to put this book together. For help with information and our interpretation of London history, thanks to Francis Shepherd, David Cannadine, F.M.L. Thompson, David Reeder, Bill Fishman, Ralph Samuel, Ken Young, John Freeborn, John Hall, Peter Hall, Jerry White, Peter England and Rodney Mace. For assistance with picture research thanks to Philippa Lewis, Caroline Lucas, Peter Jackson, Roger Colori of Vestry House Museum, Chris Ellmers of the Museum of London, Bob Hunwick of the Clerk's Provident Association, and Bob Aspinall and Roy Johnson of the Port of London Authority. For help with interviews thanks to Jon Newman of Rose Lipman Library, Mary Bissett, Caroline Scott, Libby Spencer, Terry McCarthy of the Museum of Labour History, all the newspapers – too numerous to mention – who published our appeals for people's memories, and the old people's homes and reminiscence aid groups who have helped us to track down interviewees. Thanks also to everyone who wrote to us with their memories and to everyone that we interviewed, especially Ted Harrison of Hoxton. Finally thanks are due to the London Weekend Television staff who worked with us on the Making of Modern London project.

The illustration on page 157 is reproduced by gracious permission of H.M. the Queen. Other photographs and illustrations were supplied or are reproduced by kind permission of the following: Bank of England, 31/1; Gordon Barnes, 64; Battersea Library, 74-5; Bedford Archives, 51, 61; Lady Charlotte Bonham Carter, 53; Bruce Castle Museum, 128, 146; Camden Libraries, 107, 134, 139; A.C. Cooper, 102; E.T. Archive, 23; House of Fraser, 57/1, 57/2, 58/1, 58/2, 62; G.L.C. Archives, 70-1, 104/1; Greenwich Archives, 121; Guardian Royal Exchange, 31/2, 34; Guildhall Library, 2-3, 14-15, 21, 26, 27, 30, 48, 77, 96-7, 101, 111; Hackney Archives, 145; Ted Harrison, 93; Kensington & Chelsea Library, 142-3; Kodak Museum, 84, 98; Peter Jackson, 40-41, 45, 46, 66-7, 148-9, 160/2, 160/3; Allen Lane, 119; Pippa Lewis, 56/1, 56/2; Museum of London, 29, 106, 131/2; London Transport Museum, 102, 104/2, 124; Mansell Collection, 19, 28, 60, 73, 108-9, 150/2, 155; Minet Library, 137; National Monuments Record, 112-13, May Pawsey, 63/2; Peabody Archives, 164-5, 166, 167, 168-9, 170/1, 170/2; Port of London Authority, 76, 78/1, 78/2, 82, 92/1, 92/2; Radio Times Hulton Picture Library, 33, 54, 100, 160/1, 162; George Spiller, 123; Tower Hamlets Picture Library, 80, 86, 88/1, 150/1; Vestry House Museum, 115, 117, 122, 126, 126-7, 131/1; Victoria & Albert Museum, 38, Weidenfeld & Nicolson Archives, 26, 35, 37, 63/1, 64.

INTRODUCTION

IT IS DIFFICULT to grasp now what an extraordinary city London was a century ago. By the 1880s, it had reached a size and complexity unparalleled in world history and, though it had no motor cars, London contained all the other elements of a modern metropolis. Today the world is familiar with great capitals and industrial towns which have several million inhabitants. The suburb, the commuter railway, city transport services, docklands extending over hundreds of acres, and decaying city centres are commonplace. Superficially all major modern cities seem to be very much the same.

Although London retains an atmosphere of its own and is still an extraordinary city, it is not at all as remarkable as it was at the height of the British Empire. It no longer leads the world metropolitan league table in terms of size or wealth. Architecturally it never has been the grandest nor the most elegant of cities. Its physical fabric is not even very old, though much is made in tourist brochures of its 'historic past', with the Tower of London prominently displayed.

London is essentially a modern city, in the sense that it was the first great metropolis of the industrial age. It is really this quality of the city, characterized by its miles of Victorian terraced and semi-detached housing rather than any of its surviving buildings from an earlier age, that makes London so fascinating. The pace at which it grew from a major European city, with nearly a million inhabitants in 1800, to the biggest city in the world in 1900 with over four million people was quite staggering, and it is only recently that historians have begun to piece together the true story of London's nineteenth-century expansion.

For, despite the drama of London's Victorian and Edwardian growth, there has really been much greater interest amongst historians in its more ancient past. The 'historic' Roman, medieval or Elizabethan periods have attracted more attention, and the tourist visiting London for the first time is often confronted with a peculiar sense of unease. He or she has been led to believe that this is an ancient city, which of course it is, and that much of its venerable past is still observable, which it isn't. It is probably for this reason that so many American visitors are struck first of all by the fact that London doesn't *look* half as old as they expected. The really antiquated monuments, such as Westminster Abbey and the Tower of London, are few and far between. It's true that there is also an interest in what is known as 'Dickens' London', but this tends to be a kind of treasure hunt for places that happen to be mentioned in his books rather than any real fascination with London of the nineteenth century.

The truth is that Roman London is now submerged under several feet of earth, and is exposed only during the excavation of the foundations for yet another new office block in the City. The fabric of medieval London has also more or less disappeared altogether, though the pattern of footpaths and fields that have been built over several times has often been retained with an eerie persistence. In much the same way, the old rivers of London are hidden away in drainage pipes – the Fleet, Tyburn and Wandle – and their existence is recorded only in street names.

In fact, all the 'past Londons' prior to the Georgian age have been returned to dust, and have left only monumental reminders of the long history of the city. The Great Fire of 1666 wiped out the greater part of the City of London and, though St Paul's Cathedral and other churches survive from the great rebuilding programme, most of seventeenth-century London has gone, or remains only as a few bricks hidden behind a more recent façade. Yet, interest in this vanished London persists and seems to overshadow concern with that even more extraordinary place, the London of the Empire, a great deal of which has survived both the bombs of the Second World War and the bulldozers of the post-war years.

Had the older Londons not been demolished, they would anyway have been quite small compared with the greater London of the nineteenth century. In fact, up to two hundred years ago the only part of the metropolis which was *called* London was the square mile of the City itself, within and around the old walls. Westminster was still marked on maps as a separate place, a mile to the west along the north bank of the Thames. If you go back a further century, the City of London and Westminster were more or less separate entities physically, joined by the Strand, along which grand people built their palaces. Historic London was, then, only the City, a commercial stronghold which maintained a jealous independence from the Monarch and Parliament at Westminster. This is still reflected today in the sword ceremony which takes place when the Sovereignty of the Queen in the City is formally acknowledged.

Westminster was quite a different sort of place. From the reign of Edward the Confessor in the eleventh century, the Kings and Queens of England settled here, and it became the home of Parliament and, in time, a kind of aristocratic suburb around the Royal Court. In social and economic terms, Westminster and the City were distinct; the one made laws, the other made money.

The visitor in search of the London of more than two hundred years ago will only find it, strictly speaking, in and around the old square mile of the City, and there's very little of the original buildings left. However, what can be found from that period onwards is a good deal of the Georgian suburbia built along the main roads leading into the City.

Like the seventeenth-century churches, the surviving Georgian buildings in London are both elegant and of great architectural and social historical interest. But in the nineteenth century many of them were swamped by great waves of Victorian building which represent the most dramatic period in the history of London. It was during this era that the two great centres of power and wealth – the City and Westminster – underwent extraordinary transformations laying the social and economic foundations for what became the first great metropolis of the industrialized world.

It wasn't only the tremendous speed at which London grew during the great building booms of the nineteenth and early twentieth centuries which made it unique in Europe. Unlike other major cities, it was never controlled by a single political or religious authority, so that its expansion was largely unplanned: it was 'designed' not on the drawing board but in the market place. Power in London was divided between Parliament and the City Corporation, and all local administration remained in the hands of ancient vestries and hundreds of small authorities with responsibility for such things as paving or turnpike roads. Nearly all building was speculative in the sense that a landowner and a builder between them would finance the construction of houses in the hope of letting them on the open market.

As a result, very little building in London could match the grandeur of European cities controlled by a single aristocratic, royal or church elite, despite the enormous wealth it contained. That was not London's style. There were always plans to lay out its streets according to a grand design – such as the blueprints of Christopher Wren or John Evelyn after the destruction of the Great Fire. But they were always rejected in favour of piecemeal, individualistic development. John Nash's laying out of Regent's Park and Regent Street are quite untypical of London, in that they did involve grand planning on a considerable scale. The whole enterprise was more typical in that it was modified for economic reasons, and was never finished.

In the period of its greatest expansion, London was not a metropolis dominated by royalty or the aristocracy. It was essentially commercial and middle class. And although in the Victorian era many of the houses and official buildings have pretensions to nobility, London's wealth was represented more in the quantity of buildings put up than in the splendour of particular edifices. The city described by Charles Dickens is remembered best for its reflection of the terrible poverty which eked out a living in the midst of affluence. But Dickens also captured as well as anyone the pretensions of the new middle classes who set the tone for the great part of London's development.

As the frontiers of London pushed outwards with the formation of wave upon wave of Victorian suburbs, there were no walls to confine them. London became a scattered city unlike, for example, Paris, which remained within the walls around which its great ring road, the Peripherique, now runs. This apparently formless sprawling led people to ask whether London really existed at all as a coherent city. Indeed, the urban mass of which it was made up was not officially given the name London until 1889, when the first London County Council was elected. The scattered nature of London is still one of its most remarkable features, and it is often said that the great metropolis is really 'just a series of villages'.

It's hard to imagine anything *less* like a series of villages than the districts of London, though one or two, such as Highgate or Camberwell, do retain the shape of an earlier settlement swamped in the urban growth of the nineteenth century. The social character of the districts of London is not derived, for the most part, from the rural past. It was created by the social and economic forces which drew people into the capital, pushed them out from the centre, and redistributed them as railways were built, housing was demolished, new suburbs were put up and then sank at varying speeds into decay, and London readjusted itself countless times to the pressures both of imperial wealth and industrial development. Former villages became the scene of battles for territory between the social classes, and, as suburbs, their village character could never have survived the social and economic forces of the nineteenth century.

This book, and the television series that it accompanies, is essentially about the forces which made London grow, and moulded it into a metropolis of enormous complexity. London could not, of course, have become the place it did without the great population explosion in Britain between the late eighteenth century and the First World War. Nor could it have grown had it not been able to feed itself, first of all from the market gardens which surrounded the city on good agricultural land, and later with the produce of the largest empire in the world. And there were no serious physical obstacles to its expansion – apart from the clay soil which had to be drained to make it suitable for building. All these conditions were necessary to its growth, and we have taken them as understood. But no great city can grow without wealth, and the nature of its riches inevitably has a great influence on its character. What we have tried to explore is the way in which London's unique nineteenth-century economy created its character.

We tell the story of a great manufacturing city, the leader in Britain and the world, which expended much of its money and energy making things for itself, and drawing in through its grandiose and grossly over-built dockland the lion's share in nineteenth-century imperial wealth. Although all this happened in the 'Steam Age', London remained horse-drawn until around 1910: its technology remained simple; its planning a set of market forces; and the consequences a social and political maelstrom.

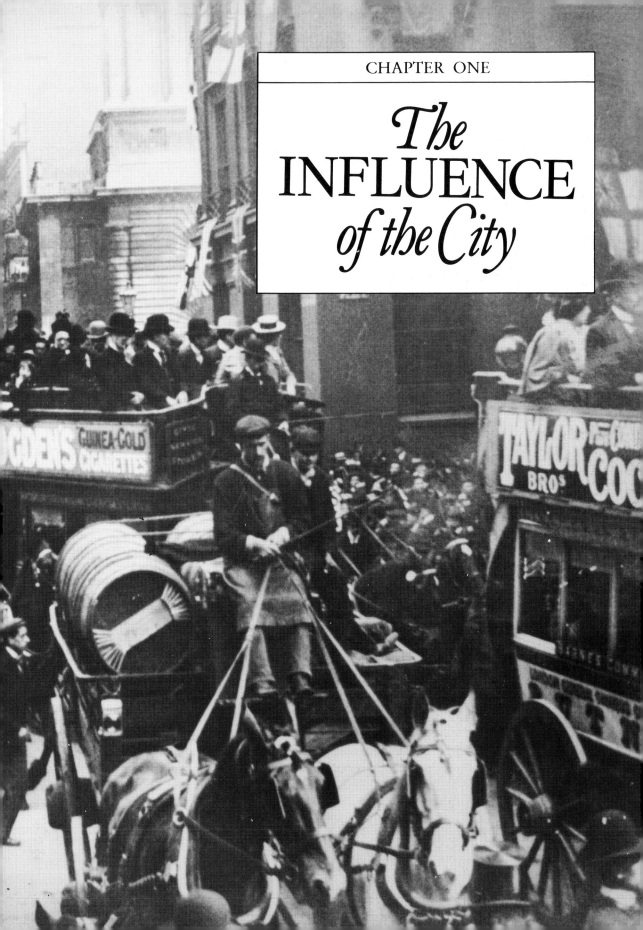

CHAPTER ONE

The INFLUENCE *of the City*

EVERYONE IN London knows about the City: it conjures up images of bowler hats and business deals. But very few people could tell you exactly what goes on there, or where the City begins and ends. Nor would they be quite sure why its civic ceremonies seem to be far more lavish and pompous than those of any other part of London, and even rival those of Royalty. In fact, images of the City are contradictory. On the one hand it symbolizes money, and a peculiarly well dressed and tidy way of acquiring very large quantities of it. On the other, its guilds and livery companies seem to be a resplendent repository of surviving ancient ritual.

The City likes to promote both images of itself. It is the dynamic centre of international finance which earns for Britain and London a vital income. Yet it is the oldest and quaintest part of the capital, the history of which is retained in its ceremony, even if most of the physical fabric of the past has been buried several times over in stone and concrete. The City cannot escape the fact of its over-riding, and still not-quite-acceptable commercialism, but it can hide behind its anachronistic ritual.

These contradictory images of the City are a reflection of its past, for it is the original site of London, a former merchant stronghold which has evolved into a crucial part of the economy of a much greater metropolis of seven million people. It has done so, in fact, not by hanging onto its past, but by a series of dramatic adjustments which have ensured that it retained the lion's share of the nation's fortune during an era of revolutionary changes in international trade and commerce. The City's ancient past and its dynamic present are graphically illustrated whenever a new building goes up in the old square mile. Archaeologists dig frantically for Roman remains in the foundations of a demolished edifice before the historic treasure is once again sealed over by a new office block.

But here we are concerned with neither the City's ancient glorious past not its modern form, but with a period in between.

In the early years of the nineteenth century, the City of London began to be transformed from a bustling centre of tradesmen, small industries, shopkeepers and wealthy merchants, with a sizeable resident population, into a square mile of financial institutions and offices. For the first half of the century its total population remained more or less stable at about 130,000, but this overall figure concealed a fundamental change. Merchants, tradesmen and shopkeepers were

Previous pages: A snarl up of bowler-hatted commuters in Cornhill in 1900, on their way to work in the City's banks, counting houses, insurance companies and money markets. In the course of the nineteenth century the City had been transformed into the business heart of London

moving out, their old premises taken over by banks, insurance offices, and financiers of various kinds. Although not a great deal is known about those who remained in the City, they were almost certainly people who were too poor to move of their own accord, and who remained in more and more crowded conditions until demolitions for new offices, roads and railways drove them out. From 1850 onwards, the population of the City plummeted, and by 1900 had fallen to 27,000. Today, there are barely 5,000 residents in the old square mile, and only the surviving steeples of the City's fine seventeenth-century churches amongst the tower blocks provide a reminder that this was once a densely inhabited area.

The start of this transformation occurred at the same time as London's growth outwards in great waves of suburban development which, by the 1870s, was to make it the largest and wealthiest city the world had ever seen. This was no mere coincidence: the two factors were governed by many of the same forces. The City was a financial power-house which was not only essential to the expansion of the metropolis but indirectly provided much of its character as well.

One of the most remarkable aspects of London as it grew in the eighteenth and nineteenth centuries was that it sprawled outwards, unconfined by any city walls, and that it grew not from one centre, but from two. The older and more important of these centres was the City of London, tracing its history back to the Romans and possibly before. The other centre, which developed from the eleventh century onwards was Westminster where the Kings and Queens of England and Parliament became established. These were originally two quite separate places, representing, in the City of London, commercial power, and at Westminster, political power.

Two hundred years ago, maps still marked the two places as distinct, although by that time they had been joined physically by building to the north of the Strand and east of Westminster. But politically the two Cities of London and Westminster retained their old distance, and a relationship of mutual dependence and distrust. The division of power between the City and Westminster was a crucial factor not only in London's development but in the way the British Empire took shape. By the end of the nineteenth century the capital was the centre of an imperial power governing a quarter of the people in the world and controlling a quarter of its land mass.

For most of its history this Empire had been essentially a commercial operation, built up by adventurers and merchants with government backing. The City and Westminster, though they were often in disagreement, had worked together to carve out new markets overseas. Merchant adventurers would get government backing for their expeditions, usually through some contact at Court, and if they were successful in finding a fruitful trade overseas they would be granted a monopoly in a particular part of the world. From the sixteenth century onwards a number of powerful chartered companies were established in this way, each with the sole right to deal in a market. The first was the Muscovy Company established when a merchant found his way to the court of Ivan the Terrible in Russia. The Hudson Bay Company, which dealt in furs and still survives today in the City, the Levant Company, and the largest of all, the East India Company, were all founded in this way.

At home, too, the City's prosperity was guarded in the seventeenth and eighteenth centuries by protective laws which gave it legal monopolies over many markets and trades. This was partly because it was believed that in order to remain economically sound a company *needed* to have a monopoly, but the City's position was made especially powerful because the Crown and Parliament frequently relied on it for funds and for men in times of war. Its charters were the reward. Thus the City controlled the main food markets, Smithfield for meat and Billingsgate for fish, and its craftsmen, such as the silk weavers of Spitalfields, were protected from foreign competition by a ban on imports. And throughout its modern history the City has managed to exact from successive governments the right to run its own affairs in its own way. When the Metropolitan Police were formed in 1829, the City got it own force; when the London County Council was established in 1889, the City remained independent.

In a sense there is no more telling a monument to the City's uniquely independent position than the Tower of London, which stands just outside the old wall to the east, dwarfed now like a toy fortress by the great glass and concrete creations of modern financial power. William the Conquerer began the building of the Tower as a show of strength to the people of London, of whom he was understandably wary. But around Guildhall today they still like to say that the Norman King never conquered *them*.

The very privileged position of the City was no more evident by the end of the eighteenth century than in the Pool of London. Here, in a ludicrously crowded stretch of the Thames, and in one or two other 'legal' quays, all ships bringing goods into London had to unload their cargo. Customs duties were amongst the City's most valuable sources of income and, despite the problems the maintenance of this monopoly created, it was reluctant to give them up. Only when the scale of pilfering from ships, forced to wait several weeks to be unloaded, seriously threatened the commercial profits of the port did the big merchant companies campaign for new and bigger docks to be built.

Around the turn of the nineteenth century, the City was finally forced to concede that existing arrangements were unworkable. The quantity of goods arriving on the Thames was increasing all the time, and sooner or later the Pool would be totally unable to cope. The City

St Paul's and Kennet Wharf, viewed from Southwark Bridge in the 1850s. Beyond the warehouses, the rows of tightly packed chimney pots show that the City was still an important residential centre at this time

authorities produced their own proposals for a new dock out in what was then a no-man's-land on the northern tip of the Isle of Dogs, well away from the East End of London, for the building of the West India Docks.

When the new West India Dock system opened in 1802, followed quickly by the London Docks on the north bank of the Thames nearer the City, and the East India Docks, the old monopoly of the City of London had been broken. Throughout most of the century the dock and wharf facilities on the Thames continued to grow in a series of competitive, cut-throat booms, and the old Pool of London lost its significance as the scale of trade grew to an unprecedented size.

The building of the new dock system in fact signalled the rapid dismantling of the ancient privileges of the City of London. Although some of the great trading companies survived, their heyday was over, and a new, much more competitive economic order swept away the monopolistic system of the previous centuries.

The City of London did not, of course, change over-night. In the first half of the nineteenth century its older leading institutions, such as the great merchant companies, were in decline, while the elements of the square mile's commercial activities that had been less significant in the eighteenth century now emerged as a new and powerful force. It's a process that still goes on, as the merchant banks – City leaders in the nineteenth century – find themselves in turn overtaken in sheer wealth and investment power by insurance companies or pension funds.

What happened in the early 1800s, and continued throughout the century was that those elements of City life that dealt in pure money, rather than goods, became immensely powerful. At the same time, the nature of the City itself changed dramatically, particularly after 1850, as its teeming urban life of shops, slaughterhouses and industries either moved out or was expelled to other parts of the metropolis. The City itself made a spectacularly successful adjustment to the pressures and needs of a new economic order in its transformation into the leading financial centre of the world. And in so doing, it provided the wealth on which much of the growth of nineteenth-century London was founded.

The strands of City life and monetary dealings are all interwoven and it is futile to search for crucial dates in its transformation: what really occurred was first a steady, then a rapid evolution in its affairs. Take, for example, dealing in stocks. In the eighteenth century, and in fact earlier, there was in the City a band of dubious characters called stock-jobbers, as well as more reputable men known as brokers. Their history and their character is rather obscure, but it is possible to say roughly what they were up to.

For there to be any stock-jobbers there have to be stocks. These are the creation essentially of a system in which a company is formed by a number of people putting money into it, entrusting its direction to some form of management, and hoping it will prosper so that their investment will produce a decent rate of interest and will increase in value. The stock-holder has a stake in the enterprise without running it.

The first of these enterprises was the sixteenth-century Muscovy Company, funded by a group of merchants who put up the money to equip ships which went in search in riches in Russia. The Bank of England, founded in 1694, operated on much the same lines. In order to raise funds for the government, this private institution attracted investments from a very large number of people – 'fund-holders' – who left the management of the Bank to its governors and hoped for a decent return on their lending. It was a way of raising very large amounts of money from a large number of people.

By the eighteenth century, there were a number of such joint-stock companies. All the merchant companies, such as the East India, the Hudson Bay, or the New River Company – which provided much of London's water supply – but, above all, the Bank of England provided a place for those who wanted to invest their money. And the stocks and funds provided a livelihood for those who would gamble on the value of them rising or falling.

East India House, home of the powerful East India Company, in Leadenhall Street in the 1800s. By this time the great merchant companies, which laid the foundations of the British Empire and generated so much of London's early wealth, were already on the decline

At that time, the stock-jobbers were men who dealt only in stocks, buying and selling them in the hope of making a profit. Brokers might also deal in stocks, but they dealt in just about everything else as well, including gold, fish and clothing. There is a long and involved history of the evolution of these two branches of what became Stock Exchange activity, but the essential point here is that, in the eighteenth century, neither jobbers nor brokers had a great deal of choice in what they dealt. Most companies were private: that is, they did not raise money – and could not unless they got special permission by Act of Parliament – by issuing shares in the enterprise; they could not have more than six members; and could not ask the general public to invest in their enterprise. The laws which restricted joint-stock companies had followed a catastrophic episode in 1720 known as the South Sea Bubble, when uncontrolled investment resulted in the collapse of the South Sea Company. In any case, the scale of eighteenth-century economic activity did not generally require massive funding. For example, all banks other than the Bank of England were private. There were plenty of them both in the City and the West End, as well as in country districts, but they were small. There were also plenty of commercial, industrial and manufacturing firms, but they, too, funded themselves privately. Similarly, there were restrictions on involvement in insurance of ships at sea – the main branch of the business in the century – and only two companies were allowed to involve themselves in it, though individuals, if they wanted, could gamble their savings on private insurance. And that is precisely what a large number of monied people chose to do.

One of the most colourful aspects of eighteenth-century London was its coffee houses. The first of these had been opened in 1652 in Cornhill in the City by a Turk named Pasqua Rosee. Rather like the fashionable Parisian café of the 1920s, the coffee house became a cultural institution and, as their numbers spread, each began to acquire a reputation with a particular clique of people, some literary, some political, some commercial. In the City of London itself there were, by the early 1700s, no less than twenty-six coffee houses as well as thirty taverns where financiers of various kinds met, mostly situated around 'Change Alley at the back of the Royal Exchange, between Cornhill and Threadneedle Street.

For the stock-jobber, later in the eighteenth century, Jonathan's and Garroways had become the most popular. Those who wanted to chip in on the insurance of a ship – which they could do as private individuals – would go to Lloyds coffee house. It was in these boisterous surroundings that the modern institutions of the Stock Exchange and Lloyds of London Insurance became established. Both took on greatly increased importance, and dealt in far greater funds in the nineteenth century, as the number of joint-stock banks multiplied.

This was an age of extraordinary industrial expansion which required massive capital investment and saw the gradual dismantling of the restrictive eighteenth-century legislation on joint-stock companies. With the coming of the railways, when for the first time very large numbers of people with small amounts of money to invest were excited by the prospect – often disastrously – the Stock Exchange came into its own. However, the City gained chiefly not by raising funds for British industry, but by 'exporting' the surplus wealth of Britain in overseas investments.

At the same time, the scale of British shipping and hence insurance expanded enormously. The Lloyds coffee-house men were in an odd position. In order to get round the eighteenth-century rule forbidding companies to insure ships at sea, they had got together as *individuals* to put up the cash to insure merchant vessels, the deal being organized by an under-writer. When, in the 1820s, the law was changed so that any company could go into the business, the Lloyds system was badly rattled. It survived, and still survives, because it had developed an information system on shipping, with agents around the world, which gave it an advance on others in terms of intelligence on insurance risks – and it always paid up. By the mid-century, it was insuring not only ships but property and all kinds of other risks worldwide.

The banking system was also transformed in the first half of the

It was eighteenth-century coffee houses like this one which spawned such City institutions as Lloyds and the Stock Exchange. Although they moved on to much grander buildings in the nineteenth century they retained –and still retain today– the noisy atmosphere of wheeler-dealing, reminiscent of the coffee house

nineteenth century. In 1824, the Bank of England lost its monopoly on joint-stock banking. The private banks were rapidly undermined as bigger operations took away their business, and in a series of amalgamations a whole new breed of joint-stock banks like Barclays, Lloyds and the Midland rose in the City, capturing the national market.

As the great merchant companies declined, there rose in London the merchant bankers. It has never been possible to distinguish absolutely between an *ordinary* bank and a merchant bank, and their activities have often overlapped. But the merchant banks, which became the wealthiest and most powerful institutions in the nineteenth century, specialized in raising money for the government and for overseas investments. In the previous century, though many merchants would also act from time to time as bankers, there had been only one merchant bank as such in the City, Baring Brothers. But between 1804 and 1839, another eleven were founded, several by Jewish financier dynasties from Europe, such as Rothschilds – the leaders – Hill Samuel, Hambros, Shroder, Brandt, Kleinwort Benson, Arbuthnot, Brown Shipley and Gibbs.

Making money out of ship insurance in Lloyd's Subscription Room, 1809. By the end of the nineteenth century merchants from all corners of the world were insuring ships, cargoes and anything that was 'high risk' at Lloyds of London

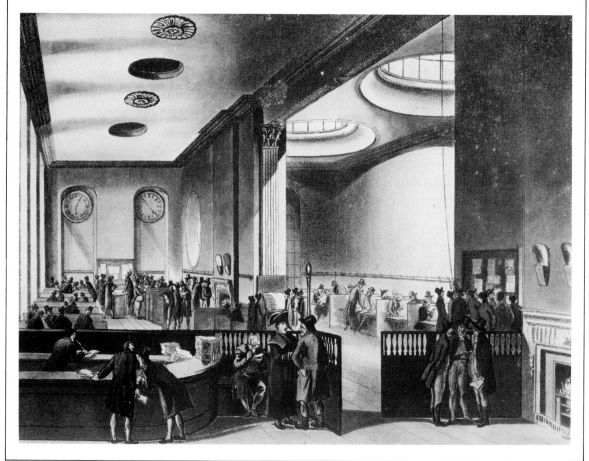

The Napoleonic Wars had created havoc and uncertainty. Rival international financial centres, in particular Antwerp, were undermined, and the City of London – while raising almost £1,000 million to fund Britain's successful challenge to Napoleon – became a haven for the international banker. And the century of peace for Western Europe which followed Wellington's victory at Waterloo provided the social and political climate in which London could operate effectively as the world's bank. It took up this opportunity with phenomenal success, investing thousands of millions of pounds in the industrialization of overseas countries, financing, for example, many labour works, mines and railways. In fact, merchant banks invested far more overseas – around £4,000 million by the end of the century, financing railways and other enterprises in the Empire – than they did in Britain. It was they who exported the capital created by the success of British industry.

If this explosion of financial activity in the old square mile is added to the rise of life insurance companies – still very few in the eighteenth century – and house insurance, the scale of monetary dealings in the City of London by 1850 was quite extraordinary. And this transformation in the foundations of wealth within the City changed not only its own internal social structure, but gave to the Greater London which grew around it a very particular kind of character which is still noticeable today.

Between 1800 and 1850, the physical appearance of the City of London itself does not appear to have changed all that dramatically. It was still largely as it had been since the rebuilding after the Great Fire of 1666, when new fire prevention regulations demanded much more use of brick and stone than had existed in medieval London. Grand planning of London along European lines, which a number of architects, including Christopher Wren, had advocated after the Fire had been rejected, so much of the old street pattern was retained, and is still discernible in the City today. The finest buildings were its churches, including, of course, St Paul's Cathedral.

The City was still a busy shopping area, on the eastern end of what had become two long avenues of stores running from the West End through the Strand to the City in the south, and along Oxford Street through to Holborn in the north. In Jane Austen's time, in the early 1800s, the City was still a place to buy all kinds of goods from drapers and others, who would live above the premises.

Wealthier merchants, who were usually distinguished from tradesmen by the fact that they dealt in foreign goods, still had their courtyard houses in the City, rather like those buildings that can still be glimpsed through doorways in European cities such as Rome or Paris.

Cloth Fair, a rack-rented City ghetto in Smithfield in the 1850s. By this time the poor were colonizing many central districts which had once housed the rich merchants, who were moving out to the suburbs

Horse-drawn traffic would daily jam the streets with terrible snarl-ups at places like the bottom of Ludgate Hill. On market days cattle and sheep were driven in from the countryside to Smithfield, where they were sold and slaughtered in a veritable Armageddon of small butcheries. Right up until 1855, when that part of the market's activities moved out to Copenhagen Fields in Islington, livestock on the hoof were regular visitors to the old square mile.

The emerging financial institutions of the City were for the first half century mostly housed in its old buildings. When, after the building of Regent Street in the West End, the City declined as a shopping district, their premises would be taken over as offices for insurance companies or some other new business. In an earlier period, the Royal Exchange itself, which had been a kind of bazaar, where all kinds of goods could be bought had been given over to dealing in commodities and stocks, until the stock-jobbers moved out – or possibly were thrown out, nobody is quite sure – into coffee houses. The first stock exchange as such was a modest affair: Jonathan's coffee house, where brokers (the relatively respectable side of the broking business) met, was burned down and a new one built, called New Jonathan's. Then, in 1773, according to *Gentlemen's Magazine* of 15 July: 'Yesterday, the brokers and others at New Jonathan's came to a resolution that instead of its being called New Jonathan's it should be called The Stock Exchange, which is to be wrote over the door'.

Smithfield Market in the 1800s. While new offices were sprouting up all over the City, right up to middle of the century thousands of animals were driven through its streets and slaughtered in a daily carnage to feed the growing metropolis

Threadneedle Street in 1898. The lines of bowlers and top hats show how by the end of the nineteenth century the City had become the demesne of the male office worker. There are no women in the shot at all

By and large, the new institutions accommodated themselves in the old fabric of the City, with perhaps abandoned merchants' houses becoming tenements for clerks, or offices, or warehouses. The City's population remained at 130,000, more or less, from 1800 to 1850, but this total figure concealed a quite sudden change in its social composition.

Greater London was growing very rapidly: from just under one million in 1800 to around two and a half millions by 1850. New districts of London that had been villages, or sometimes just open tracts of countryside and market gardens, were springing up. In the eighteenth century, on the main roads leading in to the City, lines of Georgian houses had been built by speculators catering for the City merchant's taste in a new kind of suburban living. You can still see them in Camberwell, Kennington, Hammersmith, Islington, Mile End and Hackney: elegant, flat-fronted, three- or four-storied terraces, their Georgian façades now often obscured by shop fronts.

Although there had been some movement out of the City of London after the Great Fire, when merchants took houses in the new West End squares, such as Inigo Jones's piazza in Covent Garden, the real exodus on a large scale of the wealthy from the old square mile got

under way around the early 1800s. Nobody is quite sure which kind of City person favoured which of the new suburban developments made available by landowners and speculative builders. But it is possible to provide a rough guide to the nature of this suburban exodus.

The largest group that could afford to move out of the City – in the sense that they could pay the rent on a new house, and their hours of work allowed them time to commute – would undoubtedly have been the population of clerks. These increased greatly in number as the City's financial institutions expanded, creating more and more paperwork. Before the invention of the typewriter the clerk would painstakingly produce bills and letters in hand-written script.

Not all clerks were equally well-off. Generally speaking, and this was true throughout the nineteenth century, those who worked for small businesses, the commercial clerks, were amongst the poorest, whereas those who worked in the Bank of England would be relatively comfortable. A very large number would be able to afford at least one servant, perhaps a maid of all work. The presence of a servant in the household did not mean the clerk was very high up the social scale as there was an enormous number of domestic servants in London: about 250,000 by late Victorian times. But a clerk would not be able to afford a carriage, as today someone equivalent on the social scale would almost certainly own a car. Only the very wealthy had their own means of transport. When the suburbs around the City began to grow there

George Cruikshank's famous cartoon of 'The March of Bricks and Mortar' expressed the alarm with which the rapid growth of London was viewed in the first half of the nineteenth century. Cruikshank lived in Amwell Street, Islington, and this cartoon, drawn in 1829, was a caricature of the view from his back window

A group of detached villas on Herne Hill, Camberwell in the 1820s. This was the new stockbroker belt of suburban grandeur for the well-off clerks, evidence of the growing wealth of City institutions

were no forms of public transport, other than stage-coaches, which were for the most part not designed for commuter travel and were anyway quite expensive.

So the clerkish population's suburbs grew up within walking distance of the City, principally to the north in places like Islington and Hackney, and to the south in Camberwell. There are very few records of what a clerk's life was actually like in the early nineteenth century, though there are innumerable references in the books of Charles Dickens to clerks who would walk all the way home to their semi-detached villa or terraced house in Holloway or Islington. Quite often, though he occupied with his family a whole house of a size which today seems very large, the clerk would take in lodgers, frequently a young clerk just arrived in London, in order to make ends meet. And by the end of the century, the clerk's attempt to sustain a genteel lifestyle on a similar income or less than that of an artisan was the subject of much condescending humour.

George and Weedon Grossmith's *Diary of a Nobody*, published in 1892, chronicles the daily life of a City clerk, Charles Pooter. He lived with his wife Carrie, and one servant, in a semi-detached villa called *The Laurels* in Brickfield Terrace, Holloway. The joke about Pooter – and a very snobbish one it is in its way – is that he attempts to keep up appearances in really rather shabby surroundings, and tries to lead a genteel life though tradesmen are always duping him. His social round is very dreary and he has to keep *The Laurels* in trim by his own amateurish efforts.

On the first page of his diary, Pooter proclaims:

We have a nice little back garden which runs down to the railway. We were rather afraid of the noise of the trains at first, but the landlord said we should not notice them after a bit, and took £2 off the rent.

Pooter was very much a product of the City in the sense that his social aspirations were formed there, in a working atmosphere which required punctuality, formal dress, and mixing – by working in the same institution – with the wealthy. The suburbs that were built to cater for Pooterish tastes reflect in their detail of miniature grandeur a kind of scaled-down version of the lifestyle of the wealthy. Much of the character of nineteenth-century London is derived from the fact that it was built to cater for this sort of taste. Other towns in England

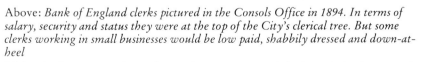

Above: Bank of England clerks pictured in the Consols Office in 1894. In terms of salary, security and status they were at the top of the City's clerical tree. But some clerks working in small businesses would be low paid, shabbily dressed and down-at-heel

Right: Studio portrait of an unknown but very Pooterish-looking clerk who worked for the Royal Exchange Assurance Company in the late Victorian period

have very similar buildings, but on nothing like the scale to be found in the inner suburbs of London.

Of course, by the time Pooter arrived on the scene in the late nineteenth century, new forms of public transport, first the horse bus, then the train and the horse tram, had carried the clerkly commuter as far afield as Ilford in Essex, so the Pooter-style suburb spread out far and wide across London. It could be found on a large scale everywhere to the north, south, and west – out in Hammersmith, Acton and Ealing, Camberwell, Peckham, Hackney and Islington. But in the middle of the century it was still those places within three or four miles of the City – considered to be a reasonable walking distance – which housed the greatest population of clerks. In fact, in some places there are streets which in the 1850s housed *nothing* but clerks: the 1851 census shows Ripplevale Grove (formerly two streets, Albion Road and Albion Grove) in Barnsbury, consisting of pretty villas, now very fashionable and 'gentrified', to have clerks, many of them City commuters, in almost every house.

But the City spawned many other, wealthier, suburbanites. There is a nice illustration of the astonishing difference in lifestyle of the average clerk and a successful speculator on the Stock Exchange, say, in the sad stories of clerks who fiddled the books at work and embezzled a fortune.

One contemporary account gives the extraordinary case of Walter Watts, a clerk with the Globe Assurance. Unlike his fellow workers, he would arrive in a carriage at the offices of the company in Cornhill. He had a house in the West End, and another in Brighton. His horses were displayed in the aristocratic parades in Rotten Row, he had a box at the opera, held magnificent banquets and became a patron of the theatre. Those who knew Watts as a wealthy man-about-town apparently had no idea where his fortune came from. All they knew was that he 'did something in the City', and it is instructive that it was not thought all that remarkable that someone with no obvious source of income should be so wealthy. Rumour had it that Watts had made his money on the Stock Exchange, or in some other form of gambling. London, in fact, was full of people with no recognizable source of income: they lived on a few investments.

It turned out that Watts was simply a £200-a-year check-clerk with the Globe, not even 'the manager with an income of £800 or £1,000 a year'. He had got his fortune by embezzlement of £70,000, and was eventually found out, sentenced to transportation and committed suicide. There were other cases of clerks who, by fraud, lived a sumptuous life for a long time without raising suspicion, the assumption being that they'd made a fortune on the Stock Exchange.

A very large number of people did make fortunes in the City without breaking the law, and they populated a rather different kind of suburb from the clerk. They might take a house on one of the main roads into London, the terraces referred to earlier, or the semi-detached villas built in the 1820s and 1840s as far away as Herne Hill or Denmark Hill in Brixton. It was this sort of City person which incensed the journalist and social reformer, William Cobbett, when he observed on his way to Croydon from Southwark 'two entire miles of stock-jobbers' houses'. Clearly Cobbett used the term 'stock-jobber' to mean City people in general, for he would have no clear idea who lived in the spreading suburbia that housed what he saw as a parasitic class. Certainly City merchants would take up such houses, and a glance at the earliest available census data – for 1841 – on, say, Brixton Hill, once lined with villas, or Denmark Hill reveals a range of inhabitants including merchants, doctors and others. John Ruskin's father, a City wine merchant, moved out to Herne Hill in the early 1800s, for example. The census returns also show a number of people describing themselves as 'Independent' or 'Fundholder', from the very large group in London who lived off the interest from government loans. In

The London to Brighton stage-coach in 1829. Even at this early period, William Cobbett noted that some City businessmen chose to live in Brighton, and commute to work on the stage-coach to Change Alley

the early part of the century there were something like 250,000 people living off 'the Funds', that is the National Debt, or borrowing by the government for the financing of State enterprises, principally war.

These people would have their own carriages to take them to and from the City, though Cobbett records people whom he calls 'stock-jobbers' travelling from Brighton to 'Change Alley in the City in the 1820s by stage-coach. In fact, before the horse bus arrived in 1829 (see Chapter Four), a network of 'short stage' coach lines had developed around London to provide a kind of commuter service. Later, areas like Paddington or Belsize Park were to develop horse-drawn commuter links with the City. The hours people worked must have been fairly short as the travelling time would not allow long periods in town. John Ruskin says that his father arrived home from the City every day at 4.30 p.m. for his evening meal.

Merchants, fundholders, stock-jobbers and brokers provided a growing custom for the new 'villa' suburbs. Tradesmen, too, who had formerly lived over their shops in the City, moved out to similar areas. It was pointed out in the 1850s that the people who dominated local politics in the City no longer lived there.

Clerks, the characteristic nineteenth-century City workers, studiously pen-pushing in the offices of the Royal Exchange Assurance Company in the 1900s

The very wealthiest City people could, of course, live the life of the English landed aristocracy, with a country mansion, and a house – or several houses – in town. The merchant bankers, who specialized in lending to governments, were by far and away the wealthiest people to

emerge from the City of London in the early 1800s. A great many of them were European Jewish dynastic families like the Rothschilds: in fact, more than half the millionaires in nineteenth-century London were Jewish.

The Rothschilds were the wealthiest and most flamboyant of the City financiers. The British branch of the family had originally established themselves as cotton merchants in Manchester, dealing with luxury goods. The merchant bank was established in the City, basing its fortune on the financing of rival armies in the Napoleonic Wars. The Rothschilds bought Gunnersbury Park in Acton in 1835 as a suburban residence, while they owned half a dozen mansions and thirty thousand acres of land around Tring and the Vale of Aylesbury, their country headquarters. In London, by the second half of the nineteenth century, they had several opulent houses in Piccadilly: Lionel Rothschild lived at 148; Ferdinand at 143; his sister at 142; and Mayer at 107. The family also had houses in Grosvenor Place, Seymour Place and Hamilton Place.

Essentially the big merchant bankers could live like the aristocracy in the West End of London, though many City people were not considered to be socially acceptable. Right up to the end of the nineteenth century new wealth based on industry and commerce was thought vulgar compared to old wealth based on landownership. Wealth derived from City finance was somewhere in between, and

New Court, the home of the Rothschild family in 1819. It was from old City houses like these that many new banks and businesses were launched. Later, they moved to purpose-built offices and the owners lived away from their businesses: the wealthiest in West End mansions and on country estates, where they sought to ape the lifestyle of the aristocracy

35

much more acceptable to the aristocracy: later in the century there was to be quite a close relationship between the City and landed wealth.

The City was also responsible to a considerable extent for the very large number of professional people in London who grew greatly in number in the nineteenth century. Districts such as Hampstead which were not essentially aristocratic like the West End, but were a cut above the middle-class suburbs, housed many lawyers, doctors and artists whose livelihood depended at least in part on City wealth.

Altogether, the emergence after 1815 of the City of London as the financial centre of the world provided the single most significant source of wealth for the growth of London. But the mass of the population were working class, and poor, however 'middle class' London's style as a city. London's population expanded partly through 'natural increase', that is the excess of births over deaths, but it was continuous immigration from the countryside which enabled it to grow at such a rapid pace. Some of these immigrants would get no further than the new suburbs, where there was a living to be made providing services as grooms, servants, or building workers. However, the poorest newcomers ended up in the most miserable housing available, in the centre.

Until the mid-century the poor could not move out of the City of London itself: new housing was much too expensive. Nothing was built for them in the suburbs, and in any case they generally had to be on hand early in the morning to go to market or to provide many of the essential services for the commuters who arrived later in the day. It was almost certain, therefore, that though the population of the City remained at roughly 130,000 from 1800 to 1850, its social composition was changing fairly rapidly. The wealthier workers had moved out, from the clerk and better-off artisan upwards, and new recruits to the City workforce at this level would settle in the suburbs when they arrived from the countryside. The poor remained trapped in the centre, in housing conditions which became more and more overcrowded.

It was from 1850 onwards that the poor were, in effect, evicted from the City by the redevelopment of the old centre, the driving through of new roads, the building of railways and railway stations, and the construction of fine Italianate office blocks for the new financial institutions of the City. The number of City residents plummeted, and by 1900 was down to 27,000.

So the transformation of the City of London itself in the nineteenth century began a pattern of suburban development and depopulation of the inner areas which was to continue in great waves well into the twentieth century. It also had a great influence on London's *style* as a metropolis, insofar as it provided a particular kind of clientele for the speculative builder who was concerned to attract, for the most part,

Bluegate Fields, Shadwell in the mid-Victorian period. As the wealthy moved out they were replaced by wave after wave of poor immigrants who were found packed into the shells of old, once grand houses, transforming them into stinking tenement slums

middle-class tenants. And none of the great expansion around the City, with the exception of the relatively careful estate management by big landowners in the West End, was really planned in any way. London was essentially a commercial city, run on commercial principles, with no single authority to oversee its expansion. The City of London itself wanted nothing to do with the administration of the suburbs to which it had given rise, and it continually thwarted the half-hearted attempts made from time to time in Westminster to do something about governing the unchecked growth of the metropolis.

Of course, not *all* of London's expansion can be explained in terms of the commercial transformation of the City itself. London was, after all, the single largest manufacturing city in the country right through the nineteenth century, although it developed little of the characteristic factory industry of the Industrial Revolution. Essentially it made things for Londoners themselves, importing far more goods through the docks than it ever exported. Many of those employed in London, including the colourful costers, flower-sellers and prostitutes described by the brilliant mid-century journalist, Henry Mayhew, got their living from a metropolitan economy which existed largely to

A Billingsgate porter, circa 1900, photographed by Paul Martin. Porters formed part of the great army of labour whose livelihood depended on the consumer demand generated by the growing metropolis

satisfy the needs of the well-to-do. And the very building of London, funded to a large extent through the accumulation of money in the City, provided an enormous amount of employment, which would not have been there had there been no demand for middle-class suburbia.

But there was one other great source of wealth for London in the nineteenth century. Though the 'new money' of the City created an expanding class of wealthy people, the landed aristocracy and gentry retained until the 1870s an overall supremacy not only in the running of the country but in terms of riches. Their wealth was derived from their estates, many of which had increased greatly in value with the Industrial Revolution and the demand for coal and minerals. The fact that London was their cultural and political centre and that they came into town for a few months every year on spending sprees formed the basis of a different kind of London economy in the West End. It is to that part of London that we go in the next chapter.

CHAPTER TWO

The West End
from Season to
Shopping Centre

IF THE CITY today is a place where tidy sums of money are made in an inscrutable way, the West End is a place where people spend money openly, conspicuously, and in large quantities. Most Londoners would describe the West End as a shopping and entertainment centre, the most fashionable part of town which puts up the wealthiest tourists and businessmen in tower block hotels along Mayfair. But where is the West End? Is it Oxford Street, Savile Row, Bond Street or Kensington High Street? Nobody is quite sure: all they know is that it conjures up images of opulence.

Much of the West End looks quite different from any other part of London: its nineteenth-century buildings are on a larger scale, and the Victorian terraces and villas are built in a stuccoed 'wedding cake' style, all the way from Bayswater and Belgravia to Notting Hill and Holland Park. Towards the centre of town the surviving old housing has been converted into smart offices with porticoed entrances, and in the smartest shopping streets, like Savile Row, the old tailors seem to be set in a kind of social aspic which delights the wealthiest tourists. A kind of West End influence spreads away westwards until it begins to crumble in the cracked stucco of North Kensington squares which sank in social esteem after they were built, or never really made it as a salubrious addition to fashionable London.

It may not be easy to define where the West End begins or ends today, but it has an unmistakable quality quite distinct from most of the other parts of London. And though its character has changed quite radically in the last century, its extraordinary past can be sensed from the scale and style of its older buildings.

Although the upper classes still have a foothold in the West End, and the young 'Sloane Ranger' whose fashionable mews cottage around Sloane Square is bought for her by daddy, provides a living link with the past, nowadays far fewer people actually live there than a hundred years ago. Today the idea that the West End was once a suburb of London – the most aristocratic and salubrious suburb of all – seems absurd. Yet in Victorian times anybody who was anybody absolutely had to have a place in Mayfair or Belgravia, principally so that they

Previous pages: Regent Street in the Season. This annual migration of aristocratic families from their country estates into town provided the driving force behind an expanding West End economy in luxury goods

could take part in what was known as the London Season. Every spring and summer the aristocracy, gentry and the wealthier merchants gathered in this part of London and in just four months spent millions of pounds on food, fashion and extravagant entertainments. A great army of labour, from footmen to fashion designers, were recruited to service them, so that by the Edwardian era almost a million people made a living, directly or indirectly, out of this West End economy. As the seasonal round drew in a wider section of society in the course of the nineteenth century, the frontiers of the West End spread westwards, and so did its influence, shaping the social and economic character of a large slice of the metropolis.

As a result of industrial and imperial expansion both the aristocracy and the new middle classes had much more money to spend than at any time before. The aristocracy had profited from their enormous landholdings by selling material rights, by collecting rents from the housing and railway building booms, and by investing their surplus thousands of pounds at high rates of interest in all corners of the Empire. And the rise of government borrowing – the National Debt – created about 250,000 'fundholders' who could live a genteel life on their investments, and thereby help to support thousands of doctors, lawyers and others.

To understand why so much of this spending power and wealth became concentrated in and around the West End, we must go back to London's pre-industrial past. A London 'Society' revolving around the Court, together with its accompanying calendar of events known as 'the Season', had existed since the time of Charles I. As Parliament increased in power and importance so the Season came to coincide to a large extent with parliamentary sessions, when upper-class MPs brought their households up to London with them. By the end of the eighteenth century the Court and Parliament were the two main forces attracting the propertied and the powerful into Westminster.

The London Season lasted for only a few months. The rest of the year was spent by the aristocracy and the landed gentry in their country seats, so that their London town houses, however grand the surviving examples in Mayfair or Belgravia may appear to us today, do not really reflect the full scale of their wealth. With the exception of such palatial mansions as the Duke of Westminster's Grosvenor House on Park Lane (demolished in the 1920s) the West End town house of the Georgian period was generally a typical London residence on a larger scale than could be found in the same period in Camberwell New Road or Upper Street Islington. There are several examples in Brook Street, Hill Street and – best preserved of all – Bedford Square in Bloomsbury.

Moreover, the process of building development in the West End was very much the same as it was elsewhere in London. The landowner would grant leases to a speculative builder, who would put up the squares, streets and terraces in the hope of letting the completed houses at a profit. Considerable control over what the builder built, and who might ultimately be allowed to rent or buy (in a few cases) the houses could be exerted by the way in which the building lease was drawn up by the landowner, and its conditions enforced by his estate staff.

But in the West End the opportunity for planned and well-controlled estate developments was much greater than in most other parts of London. This was made possible by the fact that so much of the land was held by single owners who were concerned that what was built there should remain valuable when the leases expired and full ownership of the property reverted to them. A walk around the Duke of Bedford's estate in Bloomsbury, or the Grosvenor estate in Mayfair, takes you into a well-ordered world of squares and streets set out on a grid pattern quite unlike the higgledy-piggledy medieval street pattern found in many other parts of London.

The very earliest examples of this kind of aristocratic suburban development were not in what we now think of as the West End proper. Covent Garden, for example, was laid out by the great architect Inigo Jones for the Duke of Bedford in the seventeenth century. The estate's church, St Paul's, which still survives with some original features, and the two arcaded terraces set at right angles, comprised a fashionable residential area. This was subsequently to go down hill as the piazza was taken over by market stalls and the wealthy residents moved to newer developments to the north and the west. Bedford Square, the best preserved of all eighteenth-century estate developments in London, was extremely fashionable when it was first completed in the 1770s.

But the best documented account of any West End estate covers the land owned by the Duke of Westminster in Mayfair, the Grosvenor estate which includes such famous thoroughfares as Park Lane, Brook Street, Duke Street, and, of course, Grosvenor Square itself. This has been the subject of an exceptionally detailed study by the Greater London Council's *Survey of London*.

An intriguing glimpse of life in old Mayfair in the eighteenth century is provided by a few surviving estate documents. Most of the buildings date from the 1720s onwards, and by the later part of the century it was *the* address to have in London. At that time, the parliamentary session was usually begun in November, December or January. The magazine *The World* reported in January 1790:

London is now almost at the fullest – every avenue yesterday was crowded with carriages coming into town.

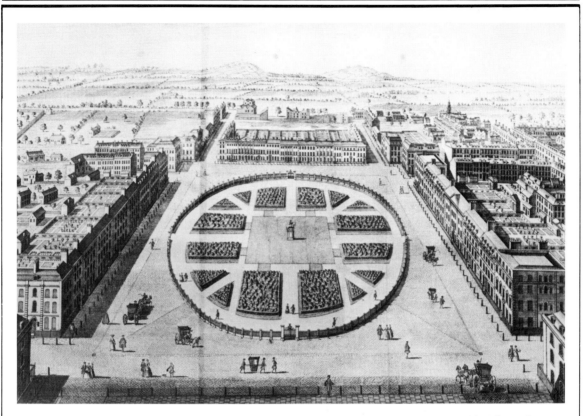

Though the calendar of seasonal events varied considerably from that of different historical periods the West End of London was always at its quietest and emptiest in the mid-summer months.

In the eighteenth and early nineteenth centuries Grosvenor Square would be almost entirely inhabited during the Season by titled families with a large retinue of servants – more than twenty in many cases. In the mid-eighteenth century, Baron Conway (later the Marquess of Hertford) kept twenty-two servants at 16 Grosvenor Street, and spent £3,000 while in London, mostly on tradesmen's bills rather than on his staff.

A remarkable survey of 1790 gives a complete social breakdown of the residents and tradesmen on the Grosvenor Mayfair estate, though it does not include the poorest classes who inhabited a slum area that had grown up just to the south of Oxford Street. In Grosvenor Square itself no less than thirty-one of the forty-seven householders were titled; and on the estate as a whole there were thirty-seven peers, eighteen baronets, fifteen 'Honourables' and thirty-nine 'Ladies'. But this was only a small proportion – less than ten per cent – of the inhabitants. Among the other residents were one or two foreign diplomats, and a number of professional people including civil servants – such as Timothy Caswell of Davies Street, a commissioner of the Salt Tax – or Court officials, such as the King's organist. There were also

A mid-eighteenth-century engraving of Grosvenor Square, one of the new developments on the lands owned by the Duke of Westminster in Mayfair. In this view, to allure upper-class tenants to lease a house on the estate, open countryside stretches northward to the rising ground of Hampstead and Highgate

army officers, doctors, architects and lawyers. But by far the largest group of residents were the tradesmen, who had shops in the area over which they lived. In fact, shops at the time were generally not purpose built, but were established in private houses. The main shopping streets were Davies Street, Duke Street, Mount Street, North and South Audley Street, Oxford Street and Park Street. All of this area – or nearly all of it – was redeveloped by the Duke of Westminster at the end of the nineteenth century in a costly late Victorian style, and the 'feel' of the place has undoubtedly changed enormously.

For example, the 1790 survey lists amongst the tradesmen fifty-five butchers who at that time would still drive livestock, bought at market, to their shops in Mayfair, where they would be slaughtered. There was a market where thirty-five butchers had their stalls, and these brought a complaint from a lady living in Brook Street. In 1801 she protested that the stable yard behind her house was so crowded on market days that she couldn't get her carriage 'aired' without running the risk of being 'gored by bullocks'. As well as the butchers, there were many other tradesmen providing food and wine, dairymen (including a cow-keeper), carpenters, bricklayers, masons, plumbers, upholsterers, cabinet-makers, dressmakers, tailors, milliners and so on.

An early Victorian traffic jam in Park Lane. Chaos was caused by convoys of cattle and sheep being driven to markets and slaughterhouses in central London. Although the rich complained about the nuisance, they helped to create it, for most of the meat ended up on their plates

In a sense, then, the West End Season provided a self-enclosed and self-perpetuating economy. Thousands of building workers were needed to put up the fine squares in which the rich lived. Houses were elegantly furnished by the cabinet-makers and master manufacturers who were concentrated around Tottenham Court Road. The family coaches would be built in Long Acre, in Covent Garden. Little luxuries, like beautifully designed barometers and clocks, kept thousands of precision metal workers in Clerkenwell busy throughout the year. Fine meals reached the tables of the rich by courtesy of a complex chain of human labour made up of dealers and traders, gangs of porters in the docks and markets, poorly paid Irish men and women who humped heavy baskets of vegetables on their heads from markets to shops, carters, shopkeepers, delivery boys, and, finally, domestic servants.

A clothing industry also arose, dependent to a significant degree upon the luxury market of affluent West End London and the Season. Every member of a rich family would have a wardrobe of expensive, tailor- or hand-made clothes for every different type of social occasion, changed and supplemented every Season according to the dictates of fashion. The most famous members of this industry were the bespoke tailors, who catered for their rich clients' whims in gentlemanly garb, and who populated the streets either side of Regent Street and on the Burlington estate. Later they congregated in Savile Row.

In the nineteenth century, this kind of economy was to expand enormously, culminating in the development of great department stores to cater for the newcomers who invaded the West End from all over London, Britain and, indeed, the world.

Not all eighteenth-century West End estates were run in quite the same way as the Grosvenor Estate, and not all would have the same social composition, but they probably had more in common with each other than with the new fashionable areas which began to develop in late Georgian times, and which spread out across the countryside and market gardens to the west of London in the Victorian period. The scale of the West End increased vastly, and became more akin to a classic Victorian suburb built on a relatively grand scale.

The single most important development marking out the West End from the rest of London in the nineteenth century was the building of Regent Street and the laying out of Regent's Park. This was a scheme devised by John Nash, the architect favoured by the Prince Regent, carved out of Crown land, though built, like everything else, as a speculation. It is about the only example to be found in London of grand planning on a scale common in European cities, and typically it was never completed and was altered not long after what had been built was finished. Nash's plan was to create on open fields in Marylebone, just north of the New Road (now Euston Road/Marylebone Road) –

Park Lane in 1895 – one of the most exclusive and desirable streets in London. Here some of the richest families in the world would own or rent a private mansion with a panoramic view across Hyde Park, using it as a base for the Season's social round

then virtually the northern boundary of built-up London – a kind of aristocratic garden city, with individual villas set in landscaped parkland. From here, there would be a broad street running down to Carlton House, providing an exclusive thoroughfare between the Park and the Prince Regent's residence.

To avoid the impression that the new Regent Street simply crossed the New Road and Oxford Street, circuses were to be built, providing elegant junctions which continued the style of the dominant thoroughfare. Regent Street, moreover, was to turn its back on London to the east – less salubrious areas such as Soho, where common mechanics lived – and to look to the west. Few roads were allowed in from the east, and the whole project was deliberately designed as a social barrier marking off the West End. Not all was finished: the fine terraces around Regent's Park certainly did become very fashionable residences, as they are today, but the circus on the New Road was only half-completed, and Marylebone Park never did get off the ground as an aristocratic suburb.

But Regent Street itself, after a faltering start, became one of *the* most fashionable haunts of London Society. As Nash had intended, it was to rival the attractions of Bond Street, with shops all the way along, and exclusive lodgings above for bachelors, beaux, and visitors to town. Butchers, greengrocers and the like were not to be allowed to trade there. Regent Street was not, in the way it is now, a main road in London: rather, it was a genuine shopping centre in which the rich could park their carriages and parade up and down, the ladies popping into shops between the fashionable hours of two and four in the afternoon, while their footmen waited outside. 'Only here,' wrote Francis Wey, a visitor in the first half of the nineteenth century, 'could you find the fashionable world so perfectly at home in the middle of the street.' And in 1866, the *Illustrated London News* contrasted the bustle of Regent Street during the Season, with its sad emptiness when the carriage class were out of town:

> In the former case, all is bustle and gaiety; in the latter, gloom and desolation. The brilliant ever-shifting scene presented daily in Regent Street during the season is dizzying in its confusion. On days of court ceremonial strings of carriages filled with beauty, rank and fashion, creep at a snail's pace towards St James's or Buckingham Palace. At other times, the fireflies of fashion glance rapidly hither and thither, and the West End streets are thronged with a promiscuous jungle of carriages, horsemen and horsewomen, cabs, omnibuses, and wagons; the pavements being crowded with fashionable loungers. With what dignified ease the gorgeously bedizened footmen attend to their mistresses or lounge about in attitudes of studied grace.

By the 1860s the extent of the West End itself, in the sense of the development of fashionable estates for the titled and wealthy, had expanded way beyond the old boundary of Hyde Park. In Belgravia, formerly a rather swampy piece of land, builders, including Thomas Cubitt, one of the greatest London builders of the century, had begun in the 1820s the development of an entirely new fashionable quarter. It was an inspirational bit of speculation, as he had recognized that the area would become attractive because of its proximity to Buckingham Palace, into which George IV moved in the 1820s. It was also close to Westminster, and was therefore likely to attract both titled and untitled Parliamentarians. The building of the Grosvenor Canal in 1823 proved also of great importance as it made feasible the transportation of building materials on a large scale, as well as the movement of a massive amount of earth required to make the site workable. Much of this infill probably came from excavations that had been made in the cutting out of the St Katharine Docks to the east of the City in the 1820s: thus a fashionable area of the West End had as its foundations the excavations of one of the developments that was to turn the East End of London into the least fashionable part of town.

At more or less the same time as Cubitt and others were developing

Belgravia, the Bishop of London's land in Paddington, a district then known as Tyburnia, was being turned into a newly fashionable suburb in a similar way. And by the 1840s, new West-End-style estates were being established square by square and street by street in Bayswater.

Some of the older West End estates to the east of Regent Street were by this time losing their fashionableness. This was true of Bloomsbury, where in 1840 Christopher Hawdy, the Bedford estate agent, noted the pull towards Belgravia and Paddington. He wrote to the Duke of Bedford: 'The great struggle not infrequently is between men in business and their wives and daughters. Their convenience would keep them here within easy reach of their places of business, but their wives and daughters would give the preference to a more fashionable address at the west or north-west end of this town.'

This suggests that City men moving westwards were to a considerable extent responsible for the demand for new housing in places like Paddington and Belgravia. From about the mid-century onwards the beginnings of a mixing of landed wealth and commercial wealth can be detected in that part of London. In fact, the shape of London, just like the social composition of Britain as a whole, was changing quite rapidly in this period. For one thing, the first railways in the north of London carved great canyons into first Euston, then King's Cross and, by the late 1860s, St Pancras, creating another social divide between east and west. Islington, which could attract the carriage trade to its shops in the 1850s, quickly went out of fashion as these three trunk lines created a twilight zone of marshalling yards and smelly steam sheds to the north of the Euston Road. At the same time, the railways – which were built to cater for long-distance rather than suburban traffic in the first instance – made the West End more accessible as a shopping area to people from the provinces. Previously they had relied on their own carriage or the stage-coach, and had been restricted to fairly short distances for shopping expeditions.

By 1850, too, the horse omnibus had become quite a feature of the West End, and the hansom cab, introduced in 1834, provided a taxi service around town for those without a carriage always at their disposal. This 'new' West End, far more extensive than in 1800, and accessible to a greater range of people, was given a tremendous boost with the staging of the Great Exhibition in Hyde Park in 1851. The number of horse buses increased to cater for the crowds, and they became an accepted part of London life, though they were still too expensive for the poorer sections of London's population.

The Great Exhibition, in effect, took the West End further west, giving rise to new fashionable developments in the old Court suburb of Kensington, which began to be built up from the 1860s onwards. As the demand for grand housing on this side of London increased, estate owners and speculative builders went to work in Notting Hill, on the

Ladbroke and Norland estates behind the older 'ribbon' development of villas and terraces which had existed since the 1820s along Holland Park Avenue. There were other districts, too, which were not quite West End, but emerged as salubrious suburbs for professionals and tradesmen who might take part in some of the fringe activities of the Season, though they were not really members of Society proper. Belsize Park and Chalk Farm were developed piecemeal from the 1840s and 1860s, forming a kind of wedge of respectability all the way from Hampstead through St John's Wood to the truly fashionable West End squares.

By this period the Season itself had grown, in the sense that more and more people seemed to be taking part in its activities. It still brought a flood of people into town, the peak in the mid-century normally being in May, June and July. Society proper continued to hold the central parts of the West End as a kind of semi-private area, with the exclusive squares often protected by gates controlled by gatemen who prevented driven cattle, buses and other 'low' traffic from passing through. The gardens in the squares were also private, as many of them are today.

   An important reason for the increase in the number of people taking

Tairton Street Gate, Bedford Square, Bloomsbury in 1893. Many estates ensured the exclusivity of high-class squares and streets by installing gates and gatemen to keep out animals, 'low' traffic and undesirables

part in the Season in the last quarter of the nineteenth century was that it provided a social introduction between the new commercial and industrial wealth of England, and the old landed wealth. Families flocked to the West End and spent thousands of pounds participating in the Season's events, principally because in so doing they gained entry into an exclusive upper-class marriage market, in which the stakes were often as high as in the money market in the City. The rush of new blood given to the Season came from upper-middle-class families of bankers, businessmen and merchants, eager for the opportunity to mix with and marry into other eligible families, preferably those with some sort of aristocratic pedigree. The comic drama of the ambitious bourgeois family apeing the aristocracy, but failing miserably to 'make it' into high Society, was not lost on contemporaries: in 1841, for example, *Punch* ran a monthly series of sketches called 'Side Scenes of Society' chronicling the social adventures and disasters of a vulgar 'nouveau riche' family, the Spangle Lacquers. And there were The Veneerings in Charles Dickens' novel, *Our Mutual Friend*.

A large part of the round of balls that were held when people were in town was to provide a social milieu in which eligible young ladies could find eligible young men. Lady Charlotte Bonham Carter, whose first Season was before the First World War, vividly remembers these occasions.

In the Season, *The Times* had an enormous list of dances each night, and I'd be invited to one more or less every night. Parents were very particular about the young men their daughters knew, and in your first year in Society you were chaperoned all the time. The mothers sat in elegant gold chairs all round the ballroom floor, whilst the daughters danced with their young men friends. Parents were very careful because they hoped that their daughter might meet a suitable marriage partner at one of these events. We would meet lots of eligible young men, a few were in the army and navy – they were always awfully nice – some from the diplomatic world, landowners, and City businessmen, young men from the City, there were masses of them, they were almost the only people one saw.

The round of seasonal events which brought people into town included the opening of Parliament, which might occur at different times but would generally be in late January, and the arrival of the Court in town at around the same time. The opera season began in mid-March, followed by State balls, the Royal Academy Exhibition, and the big race meetings, Ascot and the Derby, which were generally visited from the London house. This social round, which ended in the late summer when grouse shooting or yachting at Cowes took the fashionable people away from London, became less private as the

Lady Charlotte Bonham Carter wearing the dress in which she was presented at court in 1913

century went on. But it survived well into this century as an observable set of occasions when Society was in town, and might be seen parading in Rotten Row in Hyde Park, or queuing up in carriages in the Mall on days when debutantes were to be presented at Court, as Lady Charlotte Bonham Carter remembers.

Everyone was frightfully excited about being presented. One would arrive in the Mall, and line up and wait in one's carriage. Then one queued up, went into the beautiful throne room, and waited in line. I wore a simple white satin dress with a motif of white satin lilies, and then, of course, I had a train. A Gentleman in Waiting called out our names and first mother, then I curtsied to King George, then Queen Mary.

Every year I went to Ascot. There one went into the Royal Enclosure, but one had to send in an application first. People who had been presented at Court would automatically be allowed in when they applied. One had a special dress for that, a very smart

Rotten Row, Hyde Park in the 1890s. Every morning during the Season the fashionable world would parade up and down Rotten Row, in carriages, on horseback, or on foot, to see and be seen

garden party dress. There were only two cricket matches that were part of the Season, the Oxford and Cambridge, and the Eton and Harrow. My brother was at Eton, so we went to the Eton and Harrow, and my mother and I used to give a very jolly lunch party. One took a long table in one of the large halls in Lords, and some other friend took another table and one treated it as a kind of lunch garden party.

In the daytime the young ladies would go to Hyde Park, and there would be lots of people riding up and down Rotten Row, or walking up and down the paths talking to the riders, exchanging pleasantries and discussing events; it was most delightful. All the women rode side saddle, no female rode astride at all in those days. It was so inconvenient, in fact, the inconvenience in life, especially for women, was quite extraordinary. Then, in the evenings, people in lovely horse drawn carriages drove up and down between Hyde Park Corner and Marble Arch, and crowds of people would be walking along waving to them.

From the middle of the nineteenth century, around this Society proper in the West End, a quite new, brasher, middle-class way of life was developing. It is interesting that William Whiteley, who founded one of the most successful of the new department stores that developed in the last quarter of the century, looked at both Westbourne Grove and Upper Street, Islington when deciding the location for his new store. At the time, 1863, Upper Street was established, but Westbourne Grove, on the fringes of the West End, was hardly developed at all. However, the first Underground, the Metropolitan Line, had just opened from Paddington to Farringdon, and fashion was certainly heading in that direction. Whiteley chose Westbourne Grove, and he chose correctly, for by the end of the century the carriage trade had gone from Upper Street.

In fact, nearly all the new department stores were established in the West End, for this was now almost exclusively London's fashionable shopping district. Whereas at the start of the century, the shopping streets had run to the City in parallel lines along Oxford Street in the north, and the Strand in the south, this pattern was now well and truly broken. The City was given over more and more to commercial offices and wholesalers' warehouses.

It is interesting, too, that the new style of department store, Harrods in Knightsbridge, Whiteley's in Westbourne Grove, John Barker's in Kensington, and Tom Ponting's in Bayswater, developed in what might be called the 'new' West End. One of the principles on which they were all founded was that goods should be paid for in cash, rather than on credit, as was the custom in the old-established shops patronized by the upper classes. So the department store not only represented retailing on quite a new scale, with a single retailer selling just about every imaginable kind of item, it also broke with the conventional habits of shopping in the West End.

Most of the department stores developed from small shops, like Peter Robinsons in Oxford Street or Harrods, expanding gradually and then undergoing a major redevelopment. The new stores aimed to provide a complete day out for their customers, more and more of whom were visitors to the West End rather than local residents. Restaurants were provided, as well as 'retiring rooms' – that is, lavatories – for ladies, who could spend the day not only buying things, but reading magazines, drinking and chatting, just as men had been able to do in their West End Clubs in Pall Mall and St James's since the 1820s. Had the department stores not provided a kind of

Above: *The building of Whiteley's department store in Westbourne Grove. William Whiteley's gamble was that a quiet backwater would become a fashionable shopping centre. It paid off as, by the end of the century, Westbourne Grove, along with Kensington and Knightsbridge, had established a trendy image as the 'new' West End*

Below: *Whiteley's 'new' store just after completion. The shop expanded from drapery into, amongst other things, groceries, hairdressing, ironmongery, books and funeral undertaking. Like other shops in the area, it owed much of its success to the building of London's first Underground railway, the Metropolitan, opened in 1863, which provided easy access for shoppers*

clubroom, ladies would have been greatly inconvenienced in town: though the Ladies Lavatory Company did open its first facilities in Oxford Street in 1884, they were apparently something of an embarrassment to those who dared to use them.

By the 1880s, a day trip to the West End from the provinces was quite acceptable. As one genteel lady put it,

> Now that the train service is so perfect between London and Bath, it is quite possible to spend a day in town and return to Bath the same evening. This is no small advantage when you have a day's shopping to get through, or winter gowns and mantles to be tried on at your favourite London modistes.

Harrods Stores Limited in 1892. By the turn of the century it was London's most famous 'high-class' department store, selling everything from perfumes to pianos, and boasting that it had installed the first moving staircase (escalator) in Britain

The grocery window of John Barker's department store in Kensington High Street, 1890. Around this time the area 'took off' as a shopping centre

Right: *West End shop assistants protesting against the 'living in' system in the 1900s. Staff had to live in lodgings provided by their employers, which were often insanitary and overcrowded, and were obliged to obey petty rules and regulations controlling the little leisure time they had*

Below: *A sea of boaters, bowlers and caps as the Army & Navy Stores staff arrive for work one morning in the 1890s. They formed part of the huge army of labour employed by the West End economy*

With the arrival of yet more department stores, such as Selfridges, Liberty's, Swan & Edgar, and Debenhams, the seasonal trade of the nobility was eclipsed in the West End economy by the more continuous trade of the new middle classes. This was to include, in the fiction of *Diary of a Nobody*, the hapless Mr and Mrs Pooter from Holloway. As Alison Adburgham writes in *Shopping in Style*, 'Even they preferred to go to the West End for special purchases. It was at Shoolbred's in Tottenham Court Road that Carrie bought her 3/6d

white fan; and it was Liberty silk that made the bows she arranged at the corners of their enlarged and tinted photographs. When Mr Pooter was promoted at the office he told her "At last you shall have that little costume that you saw at Peter Robinson's so cheap." '

But the entire edifice of the West End, all the way from Mayfair to the fringes of Notting Hill, was – like a large part of the London economy – underpinned by money made elsewhere and spent in town. This really did not change dramatically as the West End grew bigger. The lifestyle of stockbrokers, landed gentry, or ex-colonials living in Bayswater did, however, require a much bigger army of poorer people; from the crossing sweeper, clearing the streets of the pollution of horse-drawn traffic, to the shop assistant; from the seamstress in the West End sweatshop, working into the night to finish a fashionable dress, to the footman in an elegant household. The big new department stores drew many new workers into the West End, where they lived mostly on the premises or in nearby hostels, run in an authoritarian manner. William Whiteley for example, was a hard master, keeping his men assistants in one set of lodgings and his women in another. Girls slept two or three to a bedroom, and they were allowed no chairs, though this was the only living space provided. Staff had to obey no less than 176 rules and could be dismissed at a moment's notice. On Sundays their lodgings were closed to them during the day, whatever the weather. Whiteley did, however, provide various clubs and societies, as well as a library – paid for by regular deductions from the assistants' salaries – which was more than most department store staff were offered.

By the standards of the time, shop assistants were not badly off: there were many other West End workers whose lives must have been miserable to an extent almost unimaginable today, and they in fact comprised the bulk of the population in many areas. Even in Mayfair today, behind the main streets which were redeveloped to a large extent in the late nineteenth century, you can find many blocks of 'industrial dwellings' – the prototype Victorian council housing, put up by philanthropists or profit-making builders of dwellings for the working classes – which replaced the old slum districts. On Chesham Buildings, just off Duke Street in Mayfair, you can see a plaque put up as an obituary to the Duke of Westminster in 1899, which reads: 'Lessor to the Improved Industrial Dwellings Company Ltd, of this and other buildings on his London Estate, accommodating hereby 4,000 persons of the working class. The friend and benefactor of his poorer brethren.'

One of the largest single sources of employment was domestic service. Moderately wealthy families might employ eleven women; including a housekeeper, lady's maid, nurse, two house maids, laundry maid, kitchen maid and scullion; and thirteen men: including a

Male servants in the 1900s: they were an important status symbol for the well-to-do, especially the footmen. Usually it was only the grandest 'carriage folk' living in the West End who could afford them

butler, valet, house steward, coachman, three grooms, two footmen, gardeners, and possibly a labourer.

Male servants, especially footmen, were a particular status symbol in the West End, but were rarely found in other parts of London. This was principally because footmen played such an important role in the Season's rituals of socializing and social climbing. They would accompany the wife and daughters on many social occasions that determined the family's social standing in Society. For example, they would escort the lady of the house on her afternoon ritual of 'calling', in which ladies called on families to follow up friendships and potentially profitable alliances, after having been introduced at social events. Footmen would also chaperone daughters at countless balls, concerts and garden parties, thus minimizing any possible mistakes that might be made on the marriage market. Families particularly valued tall, imposing footmen, and social investigator Charles Booth discovered in the 1890s that their wages varied according to their stature. A footman of 5ft 6ins could secure only £20 to £22 per annum, while one over 6ft could command between £32 and £40.

But footmen were as vulnerable as any other West End workers to the harsh laws of supply and demand which underpinned its economy. This West End luxury economy sucked in labour from the provinces or from other parts of London, primarily for the Season, then spewed them out when it had exhausted their labour power or when they were

surplus to requirements. The experience of young domestic servants provides a graphic illustration of this process. Most domestics in West London were recruited from the countryside, as they were considered to be more honest and diligent than city girls. These country girls, often innocent of the ways of the world, were particularly vulnerable to the threat of seduction by predatory city men, frequently their social superiors. Detection of pregnancy led to dismissal without a character reference, and many turned to prostitution as an alternative to destitution. Other servants turned to prostitution simply because of the seasonal nature of much domestic employment in the West End. As a result, former servants made up between a third to a half of the thousands of prostitutes in the metropolis, many of them plying their trade in the back streets east and south of the City. In fact, the prostitutes who crowded the Haymarket and other West End resorts were simply the most visible and exotic element in the peculiar economy of this part of town.

Keppel Mews South, Bloomsbury, in 1900. Today's trendy mews cottages were once home for coachmen, grooms and stable hands, who lived alongside their horses. When the rich moved out and mews fell into disuse, they were colonized by the poorest families, creating appalling slums

Women hard at work in the dressmaking department of the Army & Navy Stores in the 1890s, watched over by two male foremen. Female hands commonly worked twelve-hour days for subsistence wages in the West End at this time, and could be fired at a moment's notice

The seasonal West End economy in women's dressmaking, which employed around twenty thousand in fashion houses, many of them concentrated around Oxford Circus, Bond Street and Conduit Street, also took its toll on the workforce. During the Season dressmakers and needlewomen commonly worked twelve- to fourteen-hour days, or even seventeen hours when there were urgent Court orders. Consequently they aged very quickly and by the time they reached their thirties their fingers were no longer supple. As a result they could not work as quickly or as intricately as younger girls, and they would be dismissed, drifting eastwards to work in the slop trade of sewing and sweated labour.

However, for the many girls who willingly toiled for long hours to keep their heads above the poverty line, overwork was infinitely preferable to underwork. As May Pawsey, who was employed by a fashionable West End dressmaking house in the early part of the century, recalls, the end of the Season, signalled by the call of the lavender girls in the streets at the end of July, was a time of sorrow for it meant less work and less food in the winter months ahead.

We didn't like to hear the girls singing in the streets. They used to sing 'who'll buy my blooming lavender, sixteen branches for a penny'. We hated it because we knew that it was the end of the Season and that we would get short time. If you earned twenty-five shillings a week and they put you on three-quarter time, there wasn't much left to live on. The races, the Derby and Ascot, were very important, then it faded out because London became empty in August and they didn't want us, so they sacked the work crew.

The stark contrast between the insecurity of the poor and the opulence of the rich aroused a bitter resentment amongst some of the working-class people involved in this seasonal economy, as Edith Cox, who worked in the West End during the early part of this century, recalls.

I got a job in Hanover Square on Court dresses, and we used to do the sequin work on the dresses for the ladies who were being

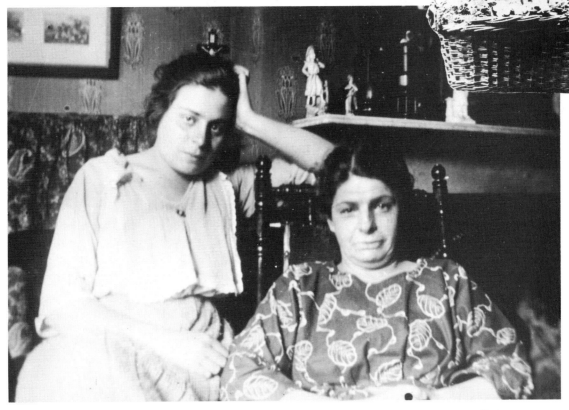

Above: *One of the many flower-sellers who crowded the West End streets every Season to earn a living*

Below: *May Pawsey and her mother in their Chelsea home in the early part of this century: 'When the end of the Season came, you never ate so well because there was no work. People would say "Oh we'll have to live off air pie now".'*

Kensington Market Court on the south side of Kensington High Street, demolished in 1869, the year after this photograph was taken. Many of the poor inhabitants of these slums provided services for the rich, but when the Season came to an end they lived on the verge of starvation

presented. There was about fourteen of us, seven either side of the table, working on each dress, and when the Court dresses were finished we were all told, 'no more work, off you go'. We used to go up to the West End every so often to see if there was any work, and if there wasn't, that was expensive paying the fare up, so we'd amuse ourselves while we were up there, and we used to go to the theatres and banquets to watch them all going in. They were all dressed up in their diamonds, jewellery and beautiful clothes, and we used to stand there, bitter, thinking to ourselves, 'fancy, they're all dressed up and there's us, we can't even get a job to live on. They don't care a hang what becomes of us.'

It wasn't just individuals but entire communities that could be plunged into poverty when the Season ended. Slum settlements sprang up as economic satellites of affluent West London suburbs in the course of the nineteenth century, four of the most squalid being the shanty town communities known as the Potteries, Notting Dale, Jennings Buildings and Kensal New Town in Kensington. Predominantly Irish, many of the inhabitants settled here after being evicted from their slum dwellings which were razed to make way for new roads, railways and shopping arteries. Hunger and disease were a serious blight in these areas and Charles Booth reported in the 1890s that in parts of Kensington over two-thirds of the people lived in poverty.

Many poor families in Kensington teetered on the verge of destitution in the winter months because the main male occupations of brickmaking, building work, street selling, market gardening and casual labouring were dependent upon the increase in demand generated by the influx of rich families for the Season in the spring and summer. For many of these families the backbreaking work of mothers and daughters as laundresses made the difference between survival and starvation. Indeed, the demand for laundresses in West London as a whole, stemming from its high concentration of wealthy households, large institutions and hotels, was so heavy that they numbered sixty thousand in the metropolis by the end of the nineteenth century. Although laundry work fluctuated with the Season, with demand declining in the winter, the all-year-round residence of many rich people in and around the West End did provide some sort of regular employment, so much so that workshop laundries honeycombed many working-class streets in West London. In Kensal New Town laundries were such a dominant feature of the landscape that it became locally known as 'Soap Suds Island', and in the mid-nineteenth century 'Laundry Land' replaced 'Piggeries and Potteries' as the popular nickname for the Potteries–Notting Dale community.

Because rich suburbs needed to be serviced, many of them were soon surrounded by colonies of workers, like those which sprung up in Kensington, housing the labouring poor, from lamplighters to laundresses and from shop assistants to sweeps. Pockets of poverty like this quickly lowered the 'social tone' of a residential area and tarnished its reputation amongst the well-to-do. Grandiose housing developments built for the rich which required extensive servicing, and thus encouraged the growth of substantial working-class communities, were particularly vulnerable to a rapid crash from aristocratic opulence to suburban seediness. This happened in Pimlico and parts of North Kensington, Bayswater and Paddington during the final quarter of the century.

Pimlico, fashionable and aristocratic shortly after it had been built in the 1840s, had thirty years later been almost deserted by the really rich, becoming a by-word for shabby gentility in London. Paddington was listed in mid-century London directories as one of the most elegant parts of town, principally occupied by aristocrats, wealthy merchants and statesmen. But from this time onwards there was a steady stream of workers and their families into the area, and soon there were slums and select residential districts side by side. Its poorest community, made up largely of building labourers, gas workers and navvies, grew up around the canal basin at the heart of the mid-Victorian suburb. As a result, Paddington was definitely passé by the 1880s, though it still retained its aristocratic quarters with their carriages and footmen.

At its core – in Belgravia and Mayfair, the better parts of South Kensington and around Bayswater – the West End residential areas managed to retain their upper-class character until the end of the century and beyond. But the fringes, North Kensington for example, were far more vulnerable to the kind of social change which affected

Shopping by gaslight in Brompton Road, 1895. Some West End shops and stores stayed open until eight or even ten o'clock in the evening which, though a bonus for shoppers, meant an eighty-hour week for some assistants

suburbs all around London. In fact, the wealthiest families responded to the ever-present threat of social decay by either moving further into town, or by moving much further out to the areas to the north-west and south, saved by the railways.

This outward push, the dispersal of fashionable 'Society people' away from the central areas, was further accelerated by the development of a new office economy in and around the West End. For, as well as being the hub of the Season's social round, areas like Belgravia and Mayfair were now becoming places where people worked in offices. Many companies established themselves in the West End because of its convenient central position and because of the high prestige enjoyed by the area. In a sense this development was simply an

extension of the whole, large-scale commercialization of the area from the mid-century onwards.

However, many of the magnificent institutional buildings which sprouted up in late Victorian times signalled something new, for they were built on a much grander scale than London was used to. The new development marked the entry of State administration into the area around the West End. In the second half of the nineteenth century there was an enormous increase in the power of the State, nourished by the expanding British Empire, and Westminster, mainly because of the need for close communication with the Houses of Parliament, became the administrative centre of operations. State intervention, for example in education and in the colonies, led to the creation of new ministries like the Department of Education and the Colonial Office, recruiting a massive number of civil servants. The establishment of the Admiralty and the War Office in Westminster at the turn of the century further increased the employment of civil servants, who numbered more than 160,000 by the 1900s. The administrators, many of them clerks, worked in grandiose government buildings around Whitehall, most of them designed in the neo-classical style, redolent of empire.

The increase in nine-to-five employment in offices around the West End also helped to shape the character of who lived where in West London, superimposing new residential patterns on top of those originally carved out by high society and the Season. Hammersmith became an area much favoured by better-off clerks, who commuted daily to work in central London on Underground trains. They lived in modest, semi-detached villas and prided themselves upon a respectable lifestyle, much lampooned in Leech's cartoons in *Punch*. Kensington, enjoying a long-established reputation for housing successful managerial and professional people, became even more thickly populated with well-heeled civil servants and administrators, who worked nearby. Bayswater, where large-scale building began in the 1850s with the erection of large town houses facing Hyde Park, attracted many families attached to the Colonial Office, and for many decades was a symbol of imperial London.

But the West End was never as completely transformed as the City: it still retains something of the air of an opulent suburb. And its style still distinguishes it from other well-heeled places in London. Socially, it has always been in a different league from Hampstead, for example, and the aristocratic wealth it brought to London provided employment for all the professional people – lawyers, doctors and artists – who lived in the suburbs one social rung down. Although it was essentially a place where the well-off spent money, it created in London an economy which was characteristic of the metropolis as a whole. The colonial officers, army chiefs, city businessmen and aristocracy made it their playground, the place they retired to, the centre of their social world, and here they disposed of the wealth they had acquired elsewhere.

The old aristocratic Season survived the First World War, and was still struggling on as a shadow of its former self in the 1950s. It has now been replaced, to some extent, by the tourist season. In the 1960s, for a brief period, London was hailed again as the world centre of a new kind of trendy fashion. 'Swinging London' was, as far as most Londoners were concerned, an odd invention of the American newspapers, taken up by Fleet Street for a while as starlets were pictured emerging with some dissolute young aristocrat or other from a West End club. In the history of this part of town, it was the sunset that the press men mistook for the dawn.

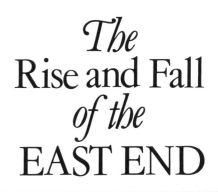

CHAPTER THREE

The Rise and Fall of the EAST END

THERE IS a great deal of sentimentality about the East End, and about the Cockney, that archetypal Londoner found behind a market stall or at the wheel of a taxi, ready with a bit of wit and wisdom on any subject. There's plenty of Cockney pride as well, with many older East Enders claiming they are true Cockneys because they were 'born within the sound of Bow Bells'. This has confused many people, especially those who go in search of that Cockney shrine, Bow Church. Quite understandably they expect to find it out along the Mile End Road, beyond Stepney and Mile End in the district of Bow. This today is typically East End, a vast expanse of small-scale industry, sad dereliction, growling lorries and new council blocks.

In fact, you won't hear the famous Bow Bells ringing in Bow, but right in the centre of the City of London, in the bell tower of St Mary-le-Bow, Cheapside, whose history goes back to the eleventh century. So the true Cockney is not somebody born in the East End at all: to be 'born within the sound of Bow Bells' is a definition of the true Londoner dating back to the early seventeenth century.

Although there is no convincing derivation of the term 'Cockney', it probably referred to the working classes of the City itself, to the colourful crowd of cab drivers, watermen, porters and others who made their living on the relatively rich pickings of the old square mile. The present rector of St Mary-le-Bow, Canon Hudson, maintains that the origins of the 'Bow Bells' Cockney pedigree was the old curfew rung in the City, which ended a night on the town for the young apprentices. The modern idea of the Cockney as someone who lives in the East End derives from the late eighteenth and nineteenth centuries, and this change in definition closely followed the change in character of the area from semi-rural to solidly working class, and the eastward drift of poor people from the central areas.

Just as we have a distinct and colourful image of the Cockney, so the East End and its history conjures up an equally distinct yet depressing image of dockland sprawl, mean streets and, most of all, poverty. This picture of poverty in the East End dates from the last decades of the nineteenth century, and it has captured the imagination as well as the

Previous pages: Providence Place, Stepney, in 1908. By the turn of the century the East End had become a by-word for poverty, slums and sweated labour

indignation of generations because it so sharply contrasts with the great wealth enjoyed by the City and the West End during the same period. For the same forces of free trade, industrialism and imperialism, which made the City and the West End spectacularly rich, created to the east of the City an expanse of poverty and wretchedness as appalling as, and in many ways worse than, the horrors of the industrial North. As the City turned into a depopulated and highly successful financial centre, serviced by the new suburbanites of Camberwell or Islington, so the East End became the site of massive dock building, of industry – particularly the most noxious manufactures, as they were expelled from the City – and of 'sweated' trades in which shoe and furniture makers and clothing workers were kept on the poverty line. Thus, the East End

A ramshackle court in Lambeth, South London, in 1870. Poverty was not confined to the East End, it also festered in the areas along the South bank of the Thames. The cobble-stones would probably have acted as a play-ground for court children, a meeting place where adults would sit and relax, and a rubbish tip

progressively lost all fashionableness as London expanded, and though it was never entirely abandoned by the middle classes, it became by the 1880s the by-word for poverty and suffering.

The East End was not always like this, and the district of Bow, out by the River Lea, which might now be thought of as classic Cockney London, was a village in 1800. Charles Dickens, as a chronicler of the seamy side of London life, rarely wrote about any person or place east of Aldgate Pump. His most desperate characters invariably emerged from the slums and rookeries of central London, such as St Giles in the Field. When Dickens was writing in the mid-nineteenth century the East End wasn't the potent symbol of urban poverty that it was to become.

In the first half of the nineteenth century places south of the Thames, like Southwark and Bermondsey, home of the leather trades and hat making, had far more of the character of manufacturing districts than did Bethnal Green or Stepney. Wandsworth, too, with its bleaching and calico industries along the River Wandle – said to be the hardest worked river of its size in the world at that time – presented more of an industrial scene than the East End.

It was the old Port of London, and shipbuilding and cottage industries that gave the East End its character. On the north bank of the Thames there was a string of hamlets from the Tower to Limehouse. These housed stevedores and lumpers who loaded and unloaded cargoes, rat catchers, ship repairers, ship's bakers, marine store dealers and watermen. The servicing of sailors provided much work for the women of Wapping and Shadwell, who would launder their dirty washing. In Limehouse there were shipbuilding yards – as distinct from cargo docks – and these, along with a thriving shipbuilding industry in Deptford, south of the Thames, supported communities of skilled sailmakers and other craftsmen.

The villages of Poplar and Blackwall were built around the East India Company's main shipyards, and the Company shaped the life of the whole community. Time was told by the Company's shipyard bell, most local people worked in the yards making and repairing East Indiamen, they worshipped at the Company chapel, their children went to the Company school, and they often ended their days at the Company almshouses.

However, the really distinctive quality of the East End at this time, which has virtually disappeared today, was its seafaring tradition stretching back many centuries. These traditions smacked of immorality and illegality, and authorities spent most of the nineteenth century trying to stamp them out. There were, for example, many

The mouth of the River Wandle, entering the Thames in 1890. By this time both sides of the Wandle had been bristling with factories and mills for many decades, helping to set parts of South London into a solidly industrial mould

The Pool of London in the eighteenth century. A forest of masts and a long tail-back of ships show how congested the old port had become and why City merchants were demanding new docks to ease the flow of traffic and trade on the Thames

disreputable lodging houses, public houses and brothels, especially along the Ratcliffe Highway in Shadwell, a sort of sailors' Regent Street which aimed to make a profit out of their shore-leave indulgences. Until the mid-century, young beaux and bloods from the West End, accompanied by their minders, would 'slum it' down the Ratcliffe Highway, watching the continuous procession of sailors and ogling at the fighting, swearing and soliciting of the prostitutes for which this street was so famous.

In fact, it was an old seafaring tradition – the bribing of crews and the pilfering of cargoes by waterside workers – which provided one important impetus leading to the building of the heavily fortified dock system that was to change the face of the East End. For by the end of the eighteenth century pilfering in the old Port of London had reached scandalous proportions. More than half a million pounds' worth of goods were stolen each year, especially from West Indiamen laden with rum, sugar and tobacco, while they were moored four or five abreast in midstream, waiting for the lighters and wherries to carry their cargoes ashore. The Thames was a pilferer's paradise because of the City's ancient restriction on imports, which specified that all cargoes should be loaded and unloaded on the quayside north of the river between London Bridge and the Tower. With the phenomenal increase in trade in the previous two centuries, this had created a bottleneck and a long tail back of ships which were frequently delayed for days or even weeks.

The volume of trade passing through London had become so great that by the late eighteenth century it was accounting for around three-quarters of all British imports and exports. Eventually the City Fathers were forced to respond to pressure from merchants to lift their old restriction, from which they had made much money out of duties, and allow new docks to be built downriver. Much of this enormous trade was controlled by the merchant companies. The most important of these was the East India Company, which had been one of the first to trade with India, China and Japan and the East Indies, and had made a fortune out of importing tea, coffee, silks, spices and sugar – all of which spawned local industries handling and processing the goods. In addition, the Muscovy Company was busy importing timber from Russia and Scandinavia, the Levant Company was importing silk and cotton from the Middle East, and the Royal African Company was heavily involved in the slave triangle.

With the lifting of the Pool of London monopoly, the London merchants involved in this overseas trade formed separate companies to build a series of docks, gigantic in both scale and cost. For they didn't just want protection against pilfering: they believed in building on a grand scale because they were confident that the Port of London was destined to achieve even greater wealth and prosperity in the new era of industrialism and international trade. In 1802 the magnificent buildings of the West India Dock rose on the Isle of Dogs between

Launch of the East India Company's ship Edinburgh *from the Blackwall Docks in November 1825. The Company's domination of London's trade and its grip on the shipbuilding villages of Blackwall and Poplar were rapidly weakening by this time*

Statue of Robert Milligan, a London merchant, in the West India Dock. Wealthy merchants like Milligan used their profits, gleaned from trade with the Empire, to mastermind the dock building that was to change the face of the East End in the nineteenth century

The building of St Katharine's Dock in 1827. It was carved out by the picks and shovels of an army of predominantly Irish navvies, assisted by hundreds of horses. By the time it was finished, London possessed by far the largest dock system in the world

Limehouse and Blackwall. This massive, fortress-like dock, half a mile in length, and big enough to accommodate six hundred ships, was surrounded with twenty-foot walls and patrolled by armed guards to prevent pilfering. Shortly after, the London Dock Company built the London Docks at Wapping, and the East India Company built the East India Dock at Blackwall. By the time the St Katharine Docks had been added hard by the Tower in 1828, London possessed by far the largest dock system in the world. The gigantic warehouses enclosing the docks and housing exotic goods from all over the Empire, rose from the riverside as a splendid monument to Britain's seafaring power. For the only time in its history, the East End and its docks were a sight that every visitor to London wanted to see.

This spate of dock building changed the whole character of the East End as the riverside area became a vast dormitory for tens of thousands of dockers and waterside workers. As they moved in, so the few middle-class people living in the area, such as merchants and retired sea captains, moved out to escape from the dirt and disease, quickly followed by company clerks, dock foremen and senior dock officials. Cottages and courts were flattened to make way for the land-hungry dock system, for the Commercial Road and the East India Dock Road built to link the docks with the City, and for street after street of jerry-built houses for dockers, labourers and their families. The whole area became set in a solidly working-class mould, with identical two-up and two-down rows of pocket-sized, Georgian-type terraces, with continuous parapet lines to hide the chimneys and roofs.

To begin with, the docks prospered. Trade steadily increased, merchant ships were discharged in a couple of days instead of a month, and pilfering was practically eliminated. Just as the City was emerging as the centre of world finance and the West End was establishing a worldwide reputation as the hub of high society, so the East End appeared to be moving towards an unrivalled position as the foremost centre of world trade, which might bring prosperity to the people of Poplar, Wapping and West Ham.

But already by the 1830s it was becoming clear to more perceptive observers that the East End expansion was built on shaky foundations and that it would not necessarily benefit from free trade as was the City. Indeed, the reverse was the case: free trade, and the competition from rival manufacturers at home and abroad that it brought in its wake, threatened to topple long-established East End industries and the domination of the Port of London itself.

Silk weaving was one of the first to be struck by free trade, and its rapid decline was a portent of the economic malaise which was later to cripple the East End. The story of the silk weavers graphically illustrates how deep-rooted East End communities with quite

A Spitalfields silk weaver at work at his loom in 1895. By this time what had once been a thriving East End industry, employing tens of thousands, had practically vanished after the lifting of customs duties had left it uncompetitive

distinctive cultures were ground down into the 'casual poor' by economic change and unemployment. Silk weaving had been carried on in London since the seventeenth century, when Huguenot refugees escaping from religious persecution in Catholic France had settled in England. Later, when it was concentrated in Spitalfields and Bethnal Green, the industry was protected by a ban on the importation of foreign finished silk fabrics. The weavers turned raw silk, which arrived from the Far East on East Indiamen, into beautiful brocades, damasks and velvets, many of which were sold in exclusive West End shops. Trade prospered so much that by the early nineteenth century they were fifty thousand strong. Many of the original weavers had a passion for music, and they would enliven the long hours they worked at their looms by singing cantatas and madrigals, or by listening to the singing birds which they were renowned for training. The community also supported a thriving Mathematical Society, formed in 1717, which possessed microscopes, telescopes and many other scientific instruments, and which was only abandoned when the silk industry fell into serious decline.

This decline began in the early nineteenth century when the lifting of customs duties on finished silks left the industry totally uncompetitive. By the 1830s, thirty thousand Spitalfields silk weavers were unemployed and on the verge of destitution. By the end of the century the industry was dead and their culture had died along with it. Silk weaving was the first in a long line of casualties, including sugar refining and the associated sack-making industry, which were crushed as soon as their life blood of monopoly and privilege were drained away.

One of the keys to the rather mystifying rise and fall of many East End industries in the era of free trade, lies in the monopolies, which until this time were enjoyed by London's merchant companies. In previous centuries City-based merchant companies, such as the East India Company, had used their connections at Court and in Parliament to gain monopolies to trade in particular products and with particular countries or continents. They had attained their power and wealth in the seventeenth and eighteenth centuries by combining a number of imperial roles: exploring new territories, forming treaties with natives, establishing plantations and mines, and developing administrative and military bases to ensure that contracts and treaties were honoured. The East India Company, for example, had a standing army of fifty thousand in India in the nineteenth century.

But the movement towards free trade gradually undermined the monopolies and privileges that had previously been enjoyed by the merchant companies. The royal monopolies granted to them in tea, coffee, sugar, and so on, were one by one withdrawn, leading to their demise by the 1850s. The wealth created by these companies was transferred more and more into banking and insurance, thereby boosting financial institutions in the City at the expense of commercial operations in the Port of London.

The great merchant companies were still a powerful force in the early 1800s, as were the companies they spawned to build docks and warehouses. But they were past their heyday, and the cut-throat competition in dock building soon began to undermine all the companies. The first, the West India and East India Dock Companies had monopolies on handling goods from their part of the world for twenty-one years. But when those monopolies were lifted in the 1820s, it was a free-for-all from which none benefited. And, though London dominated world shipping and trade, the East End and dockland foundered.

The substitution of steam for sail in the course of the century further undermined the early docks. The use of steam meant building larger ships which the older docks, seemingly built for all time and into which so much capital was sunk, were too shallow and narrow to accommodate. The desire to overcome this deficiency sparked off a further period of ruinous competition between the major dock companies who constructed the Royal Albert Dock, the West India South Dock and the Tilbury Docks in the second half of the century. London had in fact been overdocked since the first spate of competitive dock building in the 1800s, and these grandiose new schemes further outstripped the demand for deep-water dock facilities.

This constant dock building, together with the steady increase in the total volume of goods handled by the London docks resulting from the increase in international trade in the nineteenth century, makes it difficult to conceive that their relative national importance and their profitability were in serious decline. But, by the end of the century, most companies, like the East and West India Dock Companies, were forced to merge to make ends meet.

The old West India Dock gates. Although seemingly built for all time when its splendid warehouses rose alongside the river in the 1800s, by the latter half of the nineteenth century the West India Dock was proving to be a financial lame duck for, like the other early docks, it was too shallow and narrow to accommodate the new steamships. It was a product of the age of the sailing ship

Despite these setbacks the development of the docks created an enormous demand in the East End for labour. Some was skilled: the docks required coopers, ropemakers and other suppliers of equipment. Some, like the stevedores who worked on the holds of the ships, managed to carve out relatively regular work. But these were a minority: about two-thirds of dock labour was casual in the sense that there was no guarantee of work from one week to the next, and the vast majority of labourers were hired or fired on a day-to-day basis. The precarious nature of the work was a consequence of seasonal slumps in trade: China tea came in July and November; wool arrived in February and July; sugar and grain in September and April, and so on. Also, unpredictable winds and tides could delay or hasten the arrival of sailing ships by days or weeks, thus presenting the dockers with too little or too much work. In one week in 1861, 42 ships berthed in the London docks, in the next 131, in the next 209, and in the next only 29.

The availability of dock work, even though it was hard and precarious, was beginning to attract to the East End, from all corners of the world, many who were desperate for a job. In particular it lured a flood of Irish immigrants, especially in the 1840s and 1850s when they were escaping from famine in their homeland. As a result London's Irish population increased to over a hundred thousand by 1860. Many who made for the East End settled in St George's-in-the-East, Stepney and Whitechapel.

For the most part, poverty forced them to live in slums with more than their fair share of disease, drunkenness and violence. A section of the Irish population controlled key positions in the docks, as middlemen who hired and fired the casual labour and made deals with shipowners on the unloading of cargo. But many Irish simply joined the queue of displaced workers who made for the docks as a last resort.

Henry Mayhew, the mid-century social investigator, reported that 'we find men of every calling labouring at the docks. There are decayed and bankrupt master builders, master butchers, publicans, grocers, old soldiers, old sailors, Polish refugees, broken down gentlemen, discharged lawyer's clerks, suspended government clerks, almsmen, pensioners, servants, thieves – indeed everyone who wants a loaf and is willing to work for it.'

By the mid-century, then, the image of the East End was beginning to change rapidly from a seafaring centre to a seedy home of misfits, ne'er-do-wells and outcasts from all over the world. But it still had a long way to go before it became the poverty trap that gripped the late Victorian popular imagination and that, according to social reformers, was inhabited by the desperate, the destitute and the degenerate. More than anything else, it was the peculiar effect that industrialism had on the East End which accelerated the growth of a backward economy not strong enough to support the massive workforce it attracted.

The initial impact of industrialization was further to undermine the position of the London docks. The Industrial Revolution had created major manufacturing areas in the North of England which conducted their own import and export trade through more convenient and cheaper ports, like Liverpool and Hull. By the mid-nineteenth century Liverpool, for example, came to dominate the cotton trade. And while the railway, the child of the Industrial Revolution, helped to make the City and the West End rich, boosting the Stock Exchange and the Season, it sometimes had the opposite effect on the East End, and in particular the docks. For the railway quickly cornered the lion's share of the market for the internal transportation of goods that had previously been transported by sea via London.

The most crippling loss was that of coal, which had been brought to London by sea since medieval times. In the 1840s there were around seven hundred sailing colliers which regularly made the journey between the coalfields of the Tyne and Wear and London at least ten times a year. But in 1845 coal was delivered for the first time to the capital via the Great Northern Railway and, because it was a cheaper

Coal porters at work in 1887. By the last quarter of the century the railways had cornered the lion's share of the coal trade and much of what was handled on the docks was mechanized. As a result, the coal whipper who could once command high wages became a casual dock porter

and faster means of transportation, it took just twenty years to break the back of the sea coal trade.

The decline of this trade also meant less call for the chief occupation tied to it, that of the coal whipper, who was one of the aristocrats of the dockside and who earned relatively high wages to compensate for the backbreaking work and appalling conditions he endured. Coal whipping involved lifting huge sacks of coal from the hold, then at the precise moment, whipping it from ship to shore: one slight error and the whipper finished up in the water or in the hold with broken bones. The job was made even more dangerous by the thick coal dust which filled the ship's hold, contact with which led to a blackened body, choking fits and sometimes an early death. These dangers, however, were considered infinitely preferable to the prospect of being reduced to a casual dock hand, which was the fate most of London's two thousand coal whippers were faced with from the mid-century onwards, when railways and machinery for unloading coal deprived them of their jobs.

The Industrial Revolution had another fundamental and fairly unusual effect on life and labour in the East End. Artisans and small masters weren't simply swept away, as in many other parts of the country, by factories producing cheaper goods by mass-production methods. Because London was many miles away from crucial supplies of iron and coal, necessary to power steam-driven machinery, industrial innovation was costly and risky. Instead small masters, many of whom were Jews working in the cheap clothing and furniture trades in areas like Bethnal Green and Shoreditch, chose to take advantage of their proximity to the large metropolitan market and the pool of unemployed labour in the capital to pioneer their own revolution in production. This revolution, which could be easily accomplished by many East End employers with little or no capital, used not steam, but human sweat and toil, to power simple hand-driven machinery.

The origins of sweated labour are obscure, but it probably began during the Napoleonic Wars when the demand for military uniforms led the government to put contracts out to tender with middlemen. The fundamental first principle of 'sweating' was to keep costs down to an absolute minimum. It took a similar form in many industries, such as clothing, furniture-making and shoe-making, which catered for the mass consumer and retail market in the capital, from West End department stores to cheap suburban shops. The sweating system was controlled by small employers and wholesalers who sold to the shops, and they subdivided the production process into its unskilled component parts. Whereas previously a tailor invariably made a complete garment, now a different pair of hands cut, sewed by machine, sewed buttonholes, ironed and packed it. Artisans who

An East End sweatshop. Long hours of labour on the treadle machine making clothes and shoes in overcrowded workshops was the lot of generations of Jewish immigrants – a tradition which survives in the East End today with its predominantly Asian sweatshops

could not compete with the cheapness of goods produced in this way joined the labour pool of unemployed men, women and children, who had no option but to work for sub-subsistence wages.

This system began in the early 1800s but it was made more efficient and widespread by the invention in the middle of the century of simple, inexpensive hand-driven machinery like the sewing machine and the bandsaw. The work was done at home or in small, overcrowded workshops, thus keeping rent costs, which were very expensive in London, to a minimum. And the production itself was small scale. The vast majority of East End employers hired only a handful of workers. Only about a pound was needed, for example, to set up as a master tailor, and many did this by saving up their wife's earnings from domestic and laundry work. Also, many second-hand dealers became small employers. In fact, the cheap clothing trade, catering for the working classes, grew out of the Jewish-dominated second-hand clothes or 'slop trade' it replaced.

The sweating system, concentrated in Whitechapel, Bethnal Green and Stepney, was based upon gruelling sixteen-hour working days, desperate overcrowding, insanitary conditions and sub-subsistence wages. Together with work in the docks, it gave the East End much of its nineteenth-century character.

However the East End could still boast in mid-century that it possessed the most prosperous and prestigious engineering and shipbuilding industries in the land. There were four Royal Dockyards and 160 private yards in London, most of them on the section of river between London Bridge and the Woolwich Ferry. This stretch of river had since the sixteenth century equipped England with most of the battleships, merchant ships, fishing boats and barges that she needed. The yards at Blackwall, Limehouse, Millwall and Rotherhithe were famous for the quality of their work, while most of the men who worked in the London shipyards were highly skilled, eminently respectable and superior members of the working class. They often segregated themselves from other workers, living, for example, in the more exclusive New Town and Hatcham areas of Deptford, in the Maze Hill and Greenwich Park areas of Greenwich, and in the Plumstead New Town and Burrage Town areas of Woolwich.

The shipbuilding industry in London successfully adapted to the change from wood to iron and from sail to steam, for it was served by a highly inventive engineering industry, concentrated along the south bank of the Thames in Southwark and Lambeth, in which the Brunels and Robert Stephenson were leading figures.

Like the docks, the shipbuilding industry imagined it had a splendid and secure future, servicing Britain's seapower in the new age of industrialism and international trade. However, the fate of Isambard Kingdom Brunel's iron ship, the *Great Eastern*, launched at Millwall in 1857 and at the time the largest ship in the world, symbolizes the grandiose plans of the docks and its sister industries which were doomed to end in financial disaster. Thousands of tickets were sold for the launch, but the noise of the crowd prevented the many men involved in this delicate operation from hearing their commands. As a result the ship remained high and dry, and 'The Leviathan' as she was called, became the subject of many contemporary satirical cartoons. In her brief life of thirty years she was a financial failure, and when she entered the breaker's yards in 1888 the London shipbuilding industry was also practically dead.

It was knocked down, like the docks, by the double blow of industrialization and free trade. London was a long way from centres of iron and coal production, and the increasing use of high quality iron to replace wood in shipbuilding made the cost of raw materials very high. With the breakdown of merchant company monopolies and privileges previously enjoyed by the City of London, employers cut their costs in a mass exodus to Tyneside and Clydeside. This collapse brought the East End aristocracy of labour, especially mechanics, shipbuilders and sailmakers, to their knees. By 1867 there were 30,000 destitute in Poplar alone as a result of the industry's collapse, and unemployment forced them to take any casual work that was going in the docks in order to survive.

At the same time as opportunities for skilled work in reputable industries was shrinking in East London, so unskilled work in disreputable industries was expanding at a rapid pace, especially during the second half of the nineteenth century. For a very important force, contributing to the prodigious increase in people and poverty concentrated in the East End, was the entry of industries and inhabitants pushed out from central London. This exodus was a consequence of the rapid growth in the power and wealth of the City and the West End, who wished to flush out 'noxious' industries and people into other areas.

From the 1850s onwards there was a steady march of offensive trades, for whose products there was a growing consumer demand in the metropolis, into the East End heartland of Stepney and Whitechapel, and across the River Lea into areas like Bow, Old Ford and Hackney Wick. These 'stink industries', manufacturing glue from boiled blood and bones, manure, matches, rubber, soap, tar, and

Above: *Some of the Bryant & May match girls who were involved in the celebrated strike in 1888 against appalling wages and working conditions. They were just one of many groups of workers who suffered in the 'stink industries' which invaded the East End in the second half of the nineteenth century*

Below: *An East End eviction in the 1900s. When a family was turned out because they were too poor to pay the rent, they would pile up their possessions on the pavement and search for another room or two to rent in the streets nearby*

various other chemicals and products, were pushed out by high rents, by lack of space for expansion and by tighter public health regulations in the City. They found a niche in the East End because there was no body powerful enough to resist their entry and because they at least promised new jobs in a chronically under-employed community.

These sprawling industries not only scarred the local landscape but, more seriously, their chimneys spewed out a thick, obnoxious fog which discoloured houses, killed plants, contaminated the water and induced nausea amongst some of the locals. The worst polluters were the companies who manufactured manure from blood by boiling it in open cauldrons. Another serious offender was the Rothschild family who established a mint a comfortable distance from their New Court offices, but uncomfortably close to Whitechapel. The emission of sulphuric acid gas from its gold refinery was a constant cause of complaint, leading to sore throats and smarting eyes.

Those who suffered most though were the workers in these industries. In the white lead factories, which were the last resort of the starving, men were taken on by the day, and not allowed to work more than three days consecutively as the lead had such a damaging effect on their health and strength. In the Bryant & May match factory in Bow, the young women workers, who in 1888 staged the celebrated 'match girls' strike', were subjected to appalling conditions which resulted in premature baldness and 'phossy jaw' – rotting of the jawbone caused by phosphorous poisoning.

The expulsion of poor people from the central areas, many of whom gravitated to the East End either to find work or to remain fairly close to their original workplace in and around the central markets, was even more important in shaping the East End's economy of poverty. The growth of the City as a commercial and financial centre induced landlords to demolish houses and evict tenants to make way for more profitable office building. The development of the City and the West End was partly dependent upon railway links into central London, and this also led to a great loss of cheap working-class housing. Routes were chosen to pass through these areas, since they were the cheapest to purchase and demolish. In addition to this, the building and extension of docks in riverside areas and the construction of new roads feeding into the City and the West End also led to the widespread demolition of old slums. Indeed, it was a deliberate policy for new roads to cut through rookeries and slums – for example in the West End, St Giles was sliced in half by Oxford Street – in order to disperse the poor to other areas.

As a result, the poor families who were turfed out of places like Mint Street, Old Nichol Street and Lisson Grove, turned more and more of the streets in Bethnal Green, Hackney Wick and Poplar into overcrowded slums. This huge demand for accommodation in the East

End was exploited by rack-renting landlords who subdivided tenement 'doss-houses' and terraced houses so much that by the 1880s large families were often forced to live in one or two rooms, to pack four or more into each bed, and to share their toilet and washing facilities with the rest of the street. For this they would be charged an extortionate rent, which normally comprised around a quarter to a half of their weekly wage.

Despite this endemic poverty in the East End, its population continued to increase in leaps and bounds. For example, between 1841 and 1901 the numbers living in Bethnal Green rose from 74,000 to 130,000, Poplar's population increased from 31,000 to 169,000, and Stepney grew from 204,000 to 299,000. The population grew because the nature of the East End economy acted like a magnet, drawing in the destitute and the displaced not only from other parts of the metropolis but, more important, from all over Britain and the world. Many of those who arrived were poorer than those who already lived there. By the First World War there were 140,000 London Jews – most of whom had arrived from Europe as they fled persecution in the 1880s – and 140,000 London Irish.

Most of the Jewish immigrants became involved in the sweated trades, dramatically increasing the numbers working in tailoring, furniture-making and boot and shoe manufacture. Many set up their own workshops employing other Jews. Although some were successful, like Montague Burton who landed in 1901 and whose name later became synonymous with the working man's 'Sunday Best', most worked fourteen-hour-plus days for a meagre wage and lived in varying degrees of poverty. The appalling working conditions endured in the East End sweated trades are still within living memory and are graphically illustrated in the recollections of Rachael Silver, born in Stepney in 1890.*

When I first started work, I worked in houses, part of which would be used as a workshop, and we used to go around Stepney looking in house windows to see if there were any hands wanted. My first job was on trousers, doing the buttoning and the fly, that was in a house with bare walls, bare floorboards and no fire. It was freezing cold, and in the winter you'd work with all your clothes on and a scarf over your head to keep warm. Went in there at eight in the morning and you'd work right up till eight at night, doing piece work, then take home work and keep going for an hour or an hour and a half to make up your money. Sometimes the conditions were so bad you'd end up crying. Then after a few weeks or a few months you'd get the sack, there was no more work, and you'd go around looking for another job.

* Rachael Silver died in a tragic accident a few weeks after this interview.

The presence of so many Jews adding to the severe competition for a limited pool of jobs and housing aroused anti-Semitic feeling in the East End. This was expressed in minor riots against the Jews in times of panic: for example, when there were serious trade slumps; at the time of the Jack the Ripper murders in 1888 (he was popularly assumed to be a Jew); and in restrictive legislation curbing immigration in the 1900s.

Competition for jobs was made even more severe because much of the East End economy was dominated by the casual labour system of seasonal booms and slumps, in which there was regular under-employment and unemployment at certain times of the year. The real pinch came in the harsh winter months, especially January and February, when fog, rain and snow frequently brought the building industry and the docks to a complete standstill. In exceptionally severe winters, like those of 1879, 1887 and 1891, seasonal unemployment aggravated by lack of food, clothing and heating, provoked bread riots in the East End.

Some occupations were hit more severely than others: the sweated trades, for example, maintained a more constant flow of work than the docks which was one of the most insecure industries in the East End. The casual labour system in the docks revolved around a degrading scene, the 'call on' in 'the cage', enacted every morning on the quayside and encapsulating the desperate insecurity and poverty experienced in the East End. The scramble for work tickets or tallies, handed out by foremen, that it involved, continued in a diluted form into the age of containerization, and was only outlawed in the 1960s. The system is remembered by Jack Banfield, who worked on the docks in the early part of this century.

We'd have to be at the dock gates at quarter to eight in the morning for the call. This meant leaving home sometimes at six o'clock, because you had to get there early to hear the whispers, because you would need to know whereabouts on the docks the work was. So the

This casual labour system in the docks revolved around the 'call on'. The bowler-hatted foremen in the foreground chose the 'hands' they wanted for a day's work in the 1900s. Because there usually wasn't enough work to go around, many would leave hungry and despondent

Right: *A treadwheel crane, in common use on the nineteenth-century dockside, powered by six or eight men simultaneously treading the wheel round. In a day each man 'walked' the equivalent of about thirty miles*

Below: *The docks provided work for many thousands of East Enders, but this was terribly irregular and insecure, with one day in, then one day out of work*

obvious place was the tea shop or the urinal. Now you never knew whether it was going to be a half a day, one day, or a week's work. So you can imagine you have been out of work for a fortnight, how humiliating it was to present yourself like cattle for half a day's work. Medland Wharf used to have a system where they had some little brass tallies, and if they gave you a brass tally, you was employed. The thing was, when you got that brass tally in your hand, you had to grab it quick, because if you didn't what used to happen was that someone would knock it out, away would go your brass tally, and whoever picked that brass tally up got the day's work.

Of course, the fewer the ships there were to unload the more brutal the fight for the few available tickets would be: 'Coats, flesh, even ears were torn off. Men were often crushed to death in the struggle.'

Some of those who literally fought for jobs were on the verge of starvation: but most breadwinners and their families managed to survive the unemployment and seasonal slumps. They were able to do so because of massive charity handouts and because there were different seasonal cycles in different trades. For, even though there was a maximum convergence of depressed trades and hence distress in the winter months, a number of trades in fact prospered at this time. For example, the heating needs of private consumers brought much work to gas workers, sweeps and woodchoppers in the winter.

Conversely, when these trades declined in the summer, gas workers and sweeps would work on building sites or in the docks. To make ends meet – and to enjoy some fresh air – East Enders developed their own version of the seasonal migration of London Society. At the end of the summer, as many as thirty thousand casual workers and their

Ted Harrison with his family, friends and neighbours hopping in Kent in the 1900s. Ted is on the extreme right with a bandage over his eyes – the result of an accident

families left town to pick fruit in the orchards or to go 'hopping', harvesting hops in Kent, as Ted Harrison remembers:

> We used to go down to Kent every autumn, hop picking. There was mother, my granny, my sister and brother, and some friends from school. It was hard work in the fields, but we kids looked upon it as a holiday. When we used to go down hopping, they used to give us the worst bleedin' carriages; they were cattle trucks, really. We'd go about twelve at night, freezing cold, get there about three o'clock in the morning, then the gypsies would often take us to the hop houses in their carts. We'd have a box with our valuables, knife and fork, spoons, cups, oil lamps, candles, hopping pots – that was just a round pot with a wire handle, and you used to put it on the fire that you made down there, and put potatoes in there with the bacon. We used to take all our oldest clothes, then throw them all away or burn them afterwards.

For many seasonal unemployment did bring appalling hardship. Those who experienced it would often revert to street trading to earn a few pence a day, and in the late nineteenth century there were as many as fifty thousand scratching a living from the city streets during the winter months. At this time bricklayer's labourers took to hawking hot potatoes and chestnuts, whilst Irish dockers joined their wives and children selling oranges and nuts. They would push their barrows many miles searching for customers, often gravitating to fashionable suburbs like Belgravia and Paddington, where their street cries, which began at seven in the morning and continued throughout the day, provoked petitions from angry ratepayers who wanted to ban them for disturbing the peace.

The most desperate characters on the streets were those who chopped up old boxes and sold them door to door as firewood, those who were reduced to scavenging in gutters, rubbish tips and sewers, and those who chose to survive by begging rather than enter the workhouse. A few families actually starved to death, while many others were saved from destitution by mothers and children working long hours in sweated trades or, as a last resort, turning to crime or casual prostitution.

Ernest Burr was brought up in Canning Town in the early part of this century. Because his father was often away at sea and his mother turned to drink as an escape, he was left with the responsibility of providing for his younger brothers and sisters much of the time, even though he was only twelve years old:

> We were hungry and I've gone upstairs, I've looked around, nothing you could sell, because we had nothing to sell. But we used to have brass knobs on the bed and I would strip the bed of brass and take it around to the rag and bone shop, as we called it then, and I've

said to my brother, 'go out and get a half a loaf and a penn'th of jam in a cup'. They used to have the jam in a gallon jar with a big wooden spoon in it, and when you used to dip it in, the flies come out. I was the eldest and I had to look after them, see. At the finish I'd get them to go up Rathbone Street, that was the market, and fetch some orange boxes back to me, and I used to chop them up in the scullery and I used to send them out selling the wood to get some grub for us.

I was walking about with no boots and stockings on and my feet was in a terrible condition. I used to knock them on the kerbs and take no notice, and they used to have tar on the pavement and my feet would be full of tar. I used to go and get a little bit of margarine and get the tar off with it.

I used to live in a block turning, a cul-de-sac infested with rats. I remember my dad coming home on leave once and a rat came out whilst we were talking, so he said, 'What's all these holes?' So I said, 'They come out – there's no good blocking the holes up, it's not only this house, the whole street's like it'. So one come out and he trapped it with a broom and he chopped his nose off. He said, 'I'll hang it on the knocker, when the landlord comes, let him knock it off.'

It was this sort of degradation and misery which shocked late Victorian and Edwardian social investigators into promoting a picture of the East End as a kind of human dustbin overflowing with the dregs of society. There was a new awareness from the 1880s onwards that London had become a class-divided capital. The middle and upper classes in the metropolis had in the course of the nineteenth century succeeded in harnessing the forces of industrialization and imperialism to enhance their power and wealth. But in so doing, they were often ruthlessly exploitative and distanced themselves from most of the duties and obligations that they might previously have felt towards the poor by turning their back on them to live in class-segregated suburbs.

There was still, of course, appalling poverty in the West End but one reason why this was often overlooked and why the East End came to symbolize urban disintegration, and even the end of civilization in the eyes of some middle-class commentators, was because mob demonstrations and strikes by the unskilled in the last decades of the nineteenth century were concentrated in the East End. The nightmare of the powerful and the propertied was that this reserve army of the unemployed in the East End was beginning to turn traitor and to stage a riot or revolution, and to pillage the West End. This was the threat of what was called 'outcast London'.

It was a threat that was never realized, despite frequent riots throughout the century. It was, nevertheless, to shape many developments in provision for London's working-class population, and we shall be looking at these in Chapter Six.

CHAPTER FOUR

THE HORSE
and the
RAILWAY

V ERY FEW relics remain of the chief means of transport used in
the suburban development of London in the first half of the
nineteenth century. There is a horse water trough here or there; a street
in the West End and a theatre are still called the Haymarket; a few
stables survive, one converted into a flea market in Camden Town;
and, of course, many a mews in the West End has been converted into
bijou flats and houses. The horse as a means of everyday transport has
been almost forgotten. However, there are a few people alive today
whose memories go back to the turn of the century. Lady Charlotte
Bonham Carter can clearly recollect calling a cab when they were all
horse-drawn, and the awful pollution that horse-drawn traffic
produced, giving that Dickensian figure, the crossing sweeper, a very
important social function:

We often travelled in four-wheelers or hansom cabs – these were
really only for people who could afford them. The four-wheelers,
which would be going around the West End streets waiting to be
called, would be summoned by one whistle. Then there were two
whistles for the hansom, which took only one or two people. They
were adorable, with the spanking horse trotting along in front, and
they always had a bell.
But with all the horse traffic, there was an awful amount of dirt on
the streets, some of them were in a dreadful state. There were
crossing sweepers, rather oldish men, and if one gave them a coin
they would be very pleased to sweep a path across the street in front
of one. I remember once I was going to lunch with an officer from
the brigade of Guards, and I had to cross at the bottom of St James's
Street into St James's Palace where the King's Guard was, and there
wasn't a crossing sweeper. It began to pour with rain, so I rushed

*Dore's impression of
Ludgate Circus in the
1870s: a seething mass of
cabs, carts, commuters,
buses and animals being
driven to market. The
railway, paradoxically,
made the congestion in
the steets of central
London even worse*

97

Crossing sweepers in the 1900s. They performed a very important social function, clearing the roads of horse dung and rubbish, which in wet weather could quickly turn into a soggy mess that was treacherous to cross

across the street, arriving in St James's Palace looking simply frightful, my lovely white suede shoes were utterly ruined for the time being.

Nowadays, a horse in London, whether a shaggy-hoofed shire in an Easter parade in Regent's Park or a sad nag dragging a rag-and-bone cart, seems to recall a pre-industrial era rather than the Victorian 'steam age'. But that is a mistake, encouraged by an oddly blinkered view of horse power held by conventional accounts of Victorian industrialism. The nineteenth century, we are always told, was the age of the train. Railways were a revolutionary form of transport which covered long distances much faster than any vehicle the world had seen. And the assumption is made that when the railways arrived, the horse was doomed. In one, specific sense, this was true. The railways did quickly bring the end of the old long-distance stage-coach, of the coaching inns and the romance of the old roads. But off the main roads, in the countryside and in the towns, the horse not only survived the coming of the railways, it became more important than before.

This was as true of London as everywhere else. During a century in which the population of the metropolis rose from 900,000 to around six million, the Victorian suburbs were built, and London grew to cover an area eighteen miles across, hay and oats represented as important a source of fuel as coal. And in the centre of London, where there were no railways before the first Underground opened in 1863, transport remained almost entirely horse-drawn until the arrival of the motorbus and the car in the early twentieth century.

The historical importance of the horse needs to be re-emphasized. This is not because it was wonderfully efficient – which it was not – nor out of any perverse preference for animals rather than machines, but because before petrol engines and electric power it was vital to London's existence. So often the growth of London in the Victorian era is attributed simply to the coming of the railways. The common assumptions are that the suburbs could not have been built without them; that they freed London from the constraints of its old transport system; and that they brought about a revolution in everyone's perception of time and space. In fact, the horse was every bit as important as the railways right up to the early 1900s.

The railways certainly did have a dramatic effect on London. But until the 1860s, and arguably until the end of the century, their least important impact was in providing transport within London itself. And the railways certainly were not the chief reason for London's growth: no transport system could have been solely responsible for that. For suburban traffic to develop, there have to be jobs in the centre of town for people to go to, and houses built further out for them to live in. Both of these require sources of wealth, which in London were provided by the rich economies of the City and the West End. The railways did help to concentrate more and more wealth in London, and they provided many thousands of jobs, swelling London's population. But they did not create the first London suburbs.

In fact, a good deal of what was regarded in the Victorian era as suburban development pre-dates the widespread availability of even horse-drawn transport. Thousands of commuters walked from their houses in Islington or Camberwell all the way to the City. Those arriving from south of the Thames had to pay a toll on bridges which were privately owned and run. Southwark Bridge made a charge on its foot passengers until the City bought it and 'freed' it in 1856, greatly increasing this 'traffic'. In his early *Sketches by Boz*, Charles Dickens records: '. . . the early clerk population of Somers and Camden Towns, Islington and Pentonville, are fast pouring into the city . . . middle-aged men, whose salaries have by no means increased in the same proportion as their families, plod steadily along, apparently with no object in view but the counting-house. . . .'.

The establishment of these 'walking suburbs' was obviously quite feasible when the distance between the edge of built-up London and the centre was two miles or less, and people were prepared to walk. Even when buses and trains had arrived, there was often a good deal of walking to be done at the start and end of a commuter journey. In

Commuter traffic on London Bridge in 1872. Although we are accustomed to think that the railway made commuting possible, in fact, most people at this time got to work by walking or taking the horse bus

south-east London in particular, regular pedestrian short cuts were established over fields and ditches between the main roads. They were known as 'half-penny' hatches, as the owners of the land would set up a barrier and charge a toll. In fact, when London's first railway line, running along a four-mile viaduct from Deptford to Spa Road in Bermondsey, was opened, a gravel path for pedestrians was built alongside and a toll of one penny charged. In 1839, it is estimated that 120,000 people used it. Similarly, when the Rotherhithe Tunnel under the Thames was opened in 1845, it attracted 17,000 pedestrians a week: nothing like the numbers crossing the toll-free bridges, and not sufficient to make it pay, but another indication that the walking commuter was commonplace.

At the same time as the walking suburbs were being established, there were commuters who lived much further out. These were people who were wealthy enough to afford their own carriage, or the long-distance coach fares, and whose working hours were fairly flexible. A few stockbrokers lived as far away as Brighton, but more commonly the carriage folk might take up the lease on a villa in Brixton, Paddington, Clapham or St John's Wood.

So, early on, transport established a very important influence on the way in which suburbs grew, with the better-off people living a rural or semi-rural life further out, and the less wealthy confined to the districts closer to central London. Throughout the period from 1800 to the First World War, the cost and availability of transport affected the character of the London suburbs, and helped to shape social divisions. The walking commuter, with a terraced house in the suburbs, was very well-off compared with the thousands of workers trapped near the centre by their long working hours and the fact that they could never afford the rent on a new suburban home.

There was another form of transport, too, which in a restricted way had an early influence on suburban development. The Thames was not only the highway to the Port of London; for centuries it provided passenger transport services through the centre of the city. Before most of the Thames bridges were built in the eighteenth and nineteenth centuries, the river was also a barrier which could only be crossed at the behest of the watermen. In fact, in one of the earliest battles between rival forms of transport in London, the watermen had fiercely opposed the building of bridges. Many watermen survived the spanning of the Thames by road only to be faced by competition from steam-ships in the early nineteenth century.

In fact, steam-powered transport first made its appearance in London not with the railways, or the unsuccessful attempts to launch steam buses, but with the steam packets which began regular services in 1815. In the following decades they were carrying passengers as far downstream as Margate and Ramsgate. The *Observer* reported in 1837: 'The public are now able to avail themselves of the River Thames as a highway, and a healthful, safe, quick and economical conveyance between Westminster Bridge, Hungerford Market and London Bridge, by means of commodious steamboats.'

Commuters arriving for work in the City on paddle steamers in 1866, while above them the bridge, carrying the South Eastern Railway to its new terminus across the Thames at Cannon Street Station, was under construction. This steamboat commuter traffic to Gravesend, Margate and Ramsgate was soon knocked out by the railways, which proved to be much safer and speedier

A stage-coach preparing to leave Fetter Lane in the early part of the nineteenth century. The express trains steaming into Paddington, Euston and Kings Cross quickly wiped out this mode of long-distance travelling, because in a matter of hours they could speed their passengers to destinations which might have taken days to reach by stage-coach

By the 1840s, steam-boats were carrying several million passengers a year. Much of this custom was from pleasure trippers, going downriver to Greenwich Fair, for example, but there does appear to have been a considerable – and, inevitably, wealthy – commuter traffic as well. As early as 1831, an MP was claiming that Gravesend, Margate and Ramsgate had been built to cater for London commuters, though the trip to Margate took six hours by steam-boat. The river, however, was strictly limited in its potential: it provided only one route; transport suffered badly in rough weather; and steam-boats were not always 'secure, healthful and safe'. Between May 1835 and November 1838, forty-three people were drowned by steamers upsetting other craft, a dozen boats were badly damaged in collisions, and seventy-two people had to be rescued. In 1845, the *New Cricket* steam-boat exploded, killing seventeen people and injuring sixty. The real revolution in London transport lay not with coal and steam, but with hay and oats, on dry land.

Shillibeer's horse omnibus, which in 1829 operated London's first commuter bus service from Paddington – then a well-to-do suburb – to the Bank of England. Shillibeer went bust, but his idea caught on and led to a 'bus mania'

A new, more extensive and more complex pattern of commuting arose with the introduction to London of a Parisian invention, the horse omnibus. As a carriage pulled by horses, it wasn't, of course, radically different from a stage-coach, particularly the 'short stage' which operated in and around London. What was new was its ability to carry more – twelve to fifteen – passengers over short distances, its aim to provide a stopping service within town, and its cheaper fares. It was also slower than the short stage-coach, with which it competed for some years. George Shillibeer, who brought the omnibus to London, opened the first route between Paddington – then a wealthy suburb without a railway station – and the Bank of England. He had to operate in very difficult conditions. The route along the New Road (now Marylebone/Euston Road) – London's first by-pass, built in the mid-eighteenth century – was fine, but the old hackney cab drivers in the City still had a monopoly of public transport in the old square mile. Shillibeer's buses couldn't pick up or set down passengers between the City boundary and the Bank. His omnibuses were, anyway, too bulky for the narrow City streets.

But the idea caught on quickly, and other bus companies managed to succeed where Shillibeer failed. The City's hackney cab monopoly was lifted (like so many ancient City privileges) in the 1830s, during a period when there was a 'bus mania' comparable to the railway mania which had gripped the whole country. It took some time for buses to run at regular intervals, at times suitable for the commuter. And in south London, the system of turnpike roads, on which a toll had to be paid, slowed the development of regular services for some time. In fact, the turnpike trusts set up new barriers and tried to ensure all traffic was channelled along toll roads when the railways took away their long-distance traffic and their main source of revenue. By the 1850s, the turnpike trusts were desperately trying to recoup their losses by getting every penny they could from road traffic in the suburbs. A letter to *The Times* in 1850 complained that new tolls in Peckham had put a penny on the bus fare into town.

The Highgate toll gate at the foot of the Archway Road, photographed a few years before it was removed in 1876. Right up to the 1870s London's many turnpike roads, each with their own tolls and toll gates, slowed down bus services and made them more expensive

A 'knifeboard' horse bus, which seated passengers back to back on the top deck, in the 1850s. Fierce competition between the many new bus companies carrying commuters into the City led to cheaper fares, and with them the establishment of London's first public transport system. Nevertheless the fares were still way beyond the pocket of the City's working class.

Nevertheless, fierce competition between new bus companies – many of them formed, no doubt, by job-masters and coachmen whose long-distance trade had been killed off by the railways – brought fares down, and London's first public transport system was established. By 1850 horse buses were carrying commuters and day trippers from suburbs in north and west London into the City and, to a lesser extent, the West End. Each company had its own 'livery', with buses identified by their decoration rather than a number. As with nearly all Victorian private enterprise ventures, the system somehow managed to keep going, despite constant bankruptcies among those who ran the services. And, typically, fierce competition between services led to amalgamations as the weak or unlucky operators went to the wall. In 1855, the London General Omnibus Company was formed: or, rather, *La Compagnie Générale des Omnibuses de Londres*, for it was founded and owned by a group of Parisian businessmen who tried to copy in London the omnibus monopoly that existed in Paris. They failed and were never free from competition from rival bus companies.

At this time, although there was a large enough network of routes in London to constitute a public transport system, only a small section of the population could afford to hail a bus regularly or use it as a means of getting to work. Fares were high because buses were still quite expensive, and the price of their fuel remained dependent to a large extent on the English climate: a bad harvest, and hay and oats were at a premium.

But during this period, yet another new form of public transport arrived in London. From the beginning the railways were faster than buses, but the routes they could take were much less flexible, and they could not, of course, use the existing network of roads. They had to carve out entirely new channels into the growing metropolis, and presented their builders and promoters with an entirely new set of engineering, financial and political problems.

Railways excited the imagination of the age – particularly the imagination of the middle classes who could afford to use them – and, in retrospect, often appear to have been built for their own sake rather than for any clearly defined purpose. Like all other developments at the time, they were established and run by individual commercial companies and their activities were for the most part only haphazardly controlled by Parliament. It was only gradually that their impact on London was understood, and then it was never quite what had been anticipated in the flurry of activity which created them. They were certainly never planned, as were motorways in the 1960s.

It is, therefore, not all that surprising that the first railway to start operations in the metropolis was opened not between London and some other important centre of trade and commerce, but between

Deptford and Spa Road, Bermondsey. That was in February 1836; by the following December the line had reached London Bridge. It was designed to compete with the steam-boat and the stage-coach from Greenwich to central London, and its financial backers had worked out that the journey could be completed in a quarter of the time.

For most of the route, this first railway line was supported on brick arches, raising it above adjacent property. This was a device that became common to avoid the expense of closing off existing roads or demolishing buildings. The spaces beneath the arches were let off – as some still are today by British Rail – for warehouses, and even a pub. Some private houses were built in the arches, though the railway company would not allow tenants to have coal fires lest the smoke from the chimneys obscure the drivers' view, and this experiment did not prove successful.

In these respects, the London & Greenwich was typical. It was also typical that the company running the railway was never able to pay the dividend it promised, an optimistic twenty per cent: most railways struggled to make a profit. The company also anticipated a demand for cheap travel by introducing third-class fares for passengers willing to go without a seat. Much of its custom came from pleasure trippers rather than commuters: like many steam-boats on the River Thames, the railway would be busier on a holiday weekend than at any other time.

But this first London railway was untypical of later developments in

London's first railway – the London & Greenwich – in 1836. A house has been built into the arches on the right, but the railway company wouldn't allow tenants to have coal fires, lest the smoke from the chimneys obscured the driver's view

a number of ways. Not a great deal of demolition was required as most of the line ran through what had been market gardens, although the very modest London Bridge Station – not much more than a shed – did involve the removal of some slum property. Clearly the devastation, pollution and blight railways could bring to a large city were not anticipated by this line. The London & Greenwich was also novel in that it was essentially set up to compete for suburban traffic: the majority of other railways that were opened in the great boom period up to 1855 were not interested in commuters. And this first line, by pushing its terminus to London Bridge, managed to get closer to the centre of London and the City than any lines built in the north and the west. It was easier for the railways to get close to the centre from the south, where the land was not so heavily built up, and where there were fewer of the wealthier classes to resist the invasion. Although the southern lines didn't manage to cross the Thames until the second railway boom in the 1860s, London Bridge remained a useful site for a terminus and was used by several companies. The only other station opened in this early period which penetrated the centre was Fenchurch Street on the London & Blackwall line. All the other main-line stations were kept at a distance from the West End and the City.

Landed interests in the wealthier West End of London were able to resist the penetration of the railways. A Royal Commission of Metropolitan Termini, set up to monitor new projects during the mania of the 1840s, recommended that termini should be kept outside

Navvies hack out a path to take the Midland Railway into St Pancras Station in 1867. The railways destroyed thousands of poor peoples' homes and aggravated the appalling overcrowding in the central areas

the line of the New Road, London's old northern by-pass built in the mid-eighteenth century. The cost of acquiring sites in town was anyway far greater than any railway company anticipated; the further in, the more costly they were. So Euston (1837), King's Cross (1852) and Paddington (1854) began to form the familiar ring of main-line stations around northern London. The North London line (then the East and West India Docks & Birmingham Junction Railway) approached the City in a great loop through Hackney, Bow and Stepney, before arriving at Fenchurch Street.

The first major effects of the arrival of this railway network in London, as it put out feelers and shoots this way and that, were to drive canyons between one area and another; to destroy and blight a good deal of poor housing; and to cause serious traffic jams. They carried an

Blackfriars Bridge, 1885. In inner areas not served by the railways, the horse-drawn omnibus and cab remained the only forms of public transport until well into the second half of the century

increasing load of suburban traffic, beginning a process that allowed a larger number of better-off Londoners to live further out of town. But the main lines in from the north and west were not originally interested in commuters: the first station out of town on the London & Birmingham line in 1837 was at Harrow; the Great Northern's was at Hornsey; and the Great Western's was at Ealing. It wasn't until the 1860s that a large number of stations was opened along the main-line routes, serving areas which were often already built up or well on the way to development.

The railways offered some competition to the horse omnibus, but in central London and inner areas not served by the railway, the omnibus remained the only form of public transport other than the hackney cab. Moreover, the new railways greatly increased the demand for horses:

all the goods and people they brought into London had to be distributed by road. As Professor F.M.L. Thompson has eloquently put it: 'Without carriages and carts the railways would have been like stranded whales, giants unable to use their strength, for these were the only means of getting people and goods right to the doors, of houses, warehouses, markets and factories. . . . '.

In 1873, a House of Commons Select Committee set up to examine whether the country could supply sufficient horses for the demand was told by a stable-keeper: ' . . . for every new railway you want fresh horses; fresh cab horses to begin with; I know one cab proprietor, for instance, who used to keep 60 horses, and who now has 120.'

By the 1840s, there were 2,500 hackney cabs in London, a thousand more than ten years previously, while the number of buses had increased from 620 in 1839 to 1,300 in 1850. The railway companies themselves kept thousands of horses to haul their goods vehicles from depots to shops and warehouses, and there were many thousands more goods vehicles in private hands. In the same period, the number of privately-owned carriages belonging to multiplying middle classes increased rapidly.

Even before the railways arrived there had been congestion on London's streets, and a number of schemes had been hatched to cut new thoroughfares through the old fabric of the capital. In the West End there was, of course, Regent Street. In the City a start had been made on Farringdon Street, and King William Street had been cut through from the north to London Bridge in 1835. But the increase in traffic brought about by the railways, added to the need to serve a rising and increasingly wealthy population, caused severe traffic congestion. New Oxford Street was built in 1847; Victoria Street in 1851. The building of both displayed Victorian concern to combine social and traffic engineering. The extension eastwards of Oxford Street also demolished a rookery, thus removing a 'noisome neighbourhood' and replacing it with a 'spacious open street'. In the same way the line of Victoria Street was chosen as much for reasons of slum clearance as for traffic improvement. John Nash's pupil, James Pennethorn, whose scheme for the road was successful, told the Royal Commission on Metropolitan Improvements in 1845 that he had chosen the route for 'sanitary' reasons, which included 'opening communications through the most crowded parts'.

This was the conventional approach to Victorian 'improvements': the poorest housing was demolished to make way for new roads and railways. It was often the assumption, the pious wish, or occasionally the far-sighted proposal of those who thought about the matter that the homeless would be able to move out to a new suburb, and travel into work on the new forms of mass transport that were being made available. But, of course, the poor were unable to do so and the chief

Slum housing in St Giles, which was flattened to make way for New Oxford Street in the mid-century. Most Victorian road- and rail-building aimed to knock down the worst housing, making thousands home-less as no alternative accommodation was provided

effect was to increase the housing density in poor districts which remained standing.

Apart from swelling the traffic in London, which led to new swathes being cut through the grimmest parts of the centre of town, the building of railway lines and termini themselves inflicted a direct hit on the poorer parts of town. The estimates of the numbers of people thus displaced have undoubtedly been exaggerated by those who had the laudable aim of putting an end to this kind of 'improvement': some said 100,000 people had lost their homes. But even a very cautious, recent

The building of Holborn Viaduct in 1869, which was nearly a quarter of a mile in length and spanned the valley of the now enclosed River Fleet at a cost of £2½ million and 2,000 people made homeless

estimate of the destruction puts the numbers made homeless between 1857 and 1869 at 37,000, and at 76,000 for the second half of the nineteenth century.

A new spate of railway building took place in the 1860s, by which time the companies had come to understand the commercial value of the commuter and had opened many more stations closer to the centre of town. To overcome the congestion on London Bridge, Cannon Street was opened on the north bank of the Thames. This was followed shortly by a station at Holborn Viaduct – by then a road bridge across

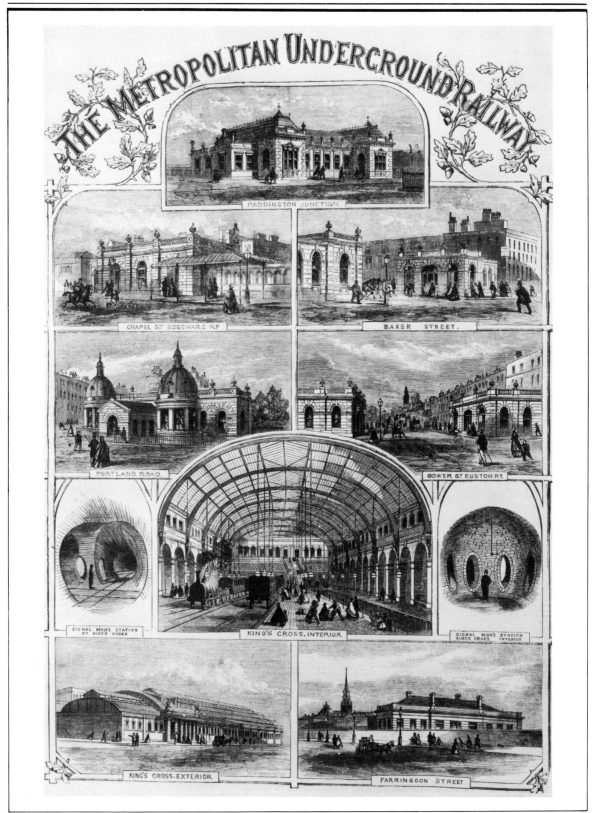

THE METROPOLITAN UNDERGROUND RAILWAY

PADDINGTON JUNCTION.

CHAPEL ST. EDGEWARE RD.

BAKER STREET.

PORTLAND ROAD.

GOWER ST. EUSTON RD.

SIGNAL MANS STATION AT KING'S CROSS

KING'S CROSS. INTERIOR.

SIGNAL MANS STATION KING'S CROSS INTERIOR

KING'S CROSS. EXTERIOR.

FARRINGDON STREET

the Fleet Valley, again built to alleviate appalling traffic congestion as horse-drawn traffic had great difficulty negotiating the steep slopes in and out of Farringdon Road.

In the north, the great monument to Victorian railway architecture in London, St Pancras Station, with its hotel, rose up between Euston and King's Cross, while Broad Street Station took the North London line right into the City. In 1863, the first underground railway in the world began to run between Paddington and Farringdon Street, and then on to Moorgate in 1865. Road traffic could no longer cope with commuter or long-distance passengers arriving at the main termini. The Metropolitan Railway was the answer, and it proved to be very successful on this, first, northern spur, though, as it was later extended to form the Circle Line, it ran into financial difficulties.

During this second great phase of railway building in London, it appears that the trains began to carry more passengers than horse-drawn vehicles, and had become the most important public transport network in the metropolis. Railways had by this period certainly allowed those who were better off to live much further out than any horse-drawn service would allow. Quite large numbers of City workers, for example, could travel in from as far away as Ealing or Harrow. Had London's transport system ceased to evolve at this point, it is difficult to know what shape the metropolis would have taken. It's possible that much larger numbers of the middle and lower middle classes would have remained in their semi-detached villas and terraces, while the working-class population remained trapped in the centre. But two new developments in the 1870s provided some escape routes for the poorer people in London, and took them out into Pooter Land.

Opposite: The Illustrated London News celebrates the opening of the Metropolitan Railway in 1863 – the first underground railway in the world – with an artist's impression of the sights and stations along the line from Paddington to Farringdon Street

Highams Park Station in north-east London. The railway provided a lifeline for this pocket of lower-middle-class commuters in 1909, while the better-off could live much further out than any horse-drawn service would allow

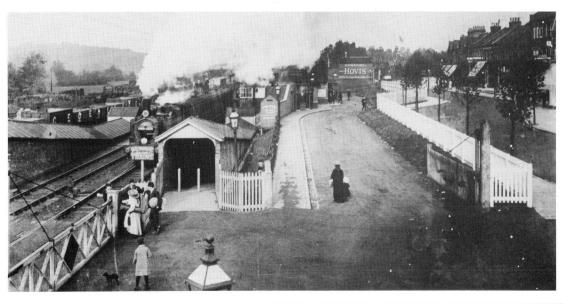

First, the horse made an extraordinary comeback. An American invention, the horse-drawn tram, began operating in London in 1870: it ran on rails, could carry more passengers than the omnibus, and was therefore cheaper. In addition, all horse-drawn transport was given a boost by the importation of cheaper grain from abroad. As the costs of road transport fell, so both buses and trams began to overtake trains in the number of passengers they carried within the built-up area of London. Whereas in 1875 buses and trams were providing 115 million passenger journeys a year and the trains between 150 and 170 million, by 1896 the position had changed. Horse-drawn transport was pulling 600 million passenger journeys, compared with the railways' 400 million. Not only did the horse overtake the train – a new pattern of transport was established.

The first, experimental horse-drawn tram was brought to London by an American called George Train. Train obviously did not understand the social geography of London because in 1861 he laid out his trial tram rails on the Bayswater Road between Marble Arch and Porchester Terrace. He had chosen the most fashionable part of town, thus raising a howl of protest from the carriage-owning classes, who could not tolerate these new vehicles hogging a fixed section of the road, on rails which stuck up above the road surface and were an obstacle to carriages. Train's tram was scrapped.

When successful tramways were established along a whole series of new routes in the early 1870s, they were not able to penetrate the West End or the City, or to get further than the railways into the intervening central area. And, although trams were more comfortable than buses, they became a working-class form of transport as they were cheaper, and had room for carrying the tools and baggage of working people.

In just four years, an entirely new and largely successful transport network of 'street railways' – the American term – had been opened in London. They ran from the Archway Tavern through Kentish Town to Euston and King's Cross; from Newington Green in Islington to Finsbury Square; from Stratford and Poplar to Aldgate; from Brixton to Westminster Bridge; from Camberwell Green through the Elephant and Castle to Southwark Bridge. The tramways were particularly strong in the inner suburbs, north, south and east of the centre. In the centre itself, buses retained their supremacy as trams were excluded.

Horse trams were much slower than trains, as vividly illustrated by Ted Harrison's memories:

> The old trams used to be drawn by two horses. To get up steep hills like Stamford Hill, they would stop, and there would be a chain horse waiting at the bottom, and they'd attach it to the front to give them extra power. Then the chain horse would be led back down to the bottom of the hill to wait for the next tram. As the tram was

going along, the driver would ring a big bell to clear the street and to warn carts in front to get out of the way. But sometimes they wouldn't and the tram would have to go very slowly, and of course there would be a real slanging match between the drivers.

When we were kids we couldn't afford the fare very often, even though it was a halfpenny or a penny, so when the conductor was upstairs or right inside, we'd jump on the back where they fastened the horses, and get a free ride. When the conductor came downstairs, we'd jump off again and run along with it until he went upstairs again: you could usually keep up – they only went at six or seven miles an hour most of the time.

A late nineteenth-century horse tram. This formed part of the new network of 'street railways' which, because of their cheapness and regularity, enabled London's working class to become commuters and to escape from the crowded central areas

But, despite this lack of speed, the horse trams had great advantages over the railways: they were cheaper, they ran frequently, and at times that suited a large section of the working-class population. Unlike the buses, trams had to provide 'cheap' workers' fares. So, in the inner suburbs they were able to compete with the trains, and allowed people

who could not previously afford it to become commuters. In 1884, the chairman of London Tramways was able to boast: 'We have relieved London of an immense number of poor people by carrying them out to the suburbs . . . building has been going on very largely on our line of roads in South London.'

This was probably one of the main reasons for the flight of the more genteel classes to suburbs further out: the working classes were moving in, splitting up the old terraced houses into multi-occupied tenements. And new, cheaper housing was being provided by speculators in the remaining spaces in the inner suburbs. London's suburban expansion had always tended to proceed in that way: the pioneers established themselves along main roads, so that building took place in 'fingers' spreading out from the centre; gradually the gaps between the fingers were filling in. By allowing a larger section of the population to become commuters, the tramways almost certainly played a part in changing the social composition of the inner suburbs, and although many lower-middle-class clerks and other low-paid workers used them, their image remained essentially working class.

Secondly, at more or less the same time another development, this time on the railways, was making it easier for the poorer classes to travel in to work. There had always been two or three classes of travel on the trains, though the companies themselves were keener to carry better-off passengers than the poor. But they were encouraged to cater for the working classes by people who felt it was wrong that the trains should benefit only the relatively well-off. It was well recognized that even with a third-class fare, the extra costs of suburban living were preventing a large section of poorer people from moving out. Lord Shaftesbury made the point that the wives of poorer families needed to remain in the centre of town for the charring and laundering jobs that provided extra income. Men with casual employment had to be in the queue early to give themselves a chance of getting a job. The extra cost of commuting, and the extra inconvenience, discouraged any movement away from the centre.

Yet the railway companies, believing that they could profit most by serving the middle and upper classes, mostly resisted pressures to introduce cheap travel as long as they could. The *Economist* was critical of this attitude as early as 1844, urging the railways to cash in on the new 'mass markets' that were emerging in consumer goods and to seek profits in quantity rather than quality. Most railway companies thought this economic nonsense. However, they were gradually forced to change their policy by legislation which gave them the responsibility of doing something for the people they made homeless by the building of new stations. The North London had to agree to provide special workmen's trains with low fares in order to get

A workman's train at Liverpool Street Station in 1884. Cheap workmen's fares in the late nineteenth century accelerated the increase in working-class commuters and the development of working-class suburbs in places like Tottenham and Walthamstow

parliamentary approval for the demolitions involved in building Broad Street Station in 1865. The Great Eastern had to do the same to get into Liverpool Street a few years later. And in 1883, a Cheap Trains Act gave railway companies in general the responsibility of providing special trains for workmen.

At first, those travelling on these trains had to 'prove' they were working class by giving their employer's name and address and details of their job. But the system eventually settled down to one in which anyone travelling before a certain time in the morning could get a cheap ticket. Workmen's fares began to succeed where third-class tickets had failed: thousands of poorer Londoners began to use them.

The value they got for their fare varied, however, from one railway company to another. In 1905, the Royal Commission on Traffic in London estimated that a two-penny workman's fare would take a passenger less than three miles on the London & North Western, the Midland, the London & South Western, and the London Brighton & South Coast. But it bought a journey of over seven miles on the South Eastern & Chatham, and nearly eleven miles on the Great Eastern. To what extent this affected the distribution of working-class commuters around London is not certain, but to the north and east, new 'working-class' suburbs began to emerge, and the movement in these directions was more noticeable than in the north-west.

The workmen's fares were, moreover, according to contemporary observers, having the same sort of effect on middle-class suburbs as the horse tram. 'Wherever you locate the workmen in large numbers,' the manager of the Great Eastern said in the 1880s, 'you utterly destroy that neighbourhood for ordinary passenger traffic. Take, for instance, the neighbourhood of Stamford Hill, Tottenham and Edmonton. That used to be a very nice neighbourhood . . . but very soon after this obligation was put upon the Great Eastern Company . . . of issuing workmen's tickets . . . the district is given up entirely, I may say now, to the working man.'

By the turn of the century, the availability of workmen's fares was also affecting south London to a considerable extent. About a quarter of the total number of suburban fares were workmen's tickets. In the inner area, six to eight miles from the centre, the proportion was much higher: forty per cent. The arrival of the working classes again hastened the flight of the middle classes, who could afford the time and the money to live further out.

The growth of London's transport system, from the steam-boats and horse omnibuses to the railways and horse trams, with their workmen's fares, obviously had a powerful influence on the way in which districts rose and declined. But these effects were not simply confined to the ways in which the system prevented or enabled people to move out of the city centre.

Throughout the second half of the nineteenth century, London's population was growing at an astonishing pace: the number of people in a suburb could increase ten-fold in fifteen or twenty years. Quite a large part of this increase resulted from people moving *into* London from the surrounding towns and villages, so that the social composition of any suburb was not dependent on the sort of people who had moved out of the centre of town. It was really a matter of what sort of person could be attracted from both inside and outside London, and once a suburb was established, it quickly took on a life of its own, providing more employment for people locally than was available in town for those who commuted. Generally speaking, it was the wealthier suburbs which required the largest workforce of domestics, tradesmen of all kinds, grooms and other stable-workers, delivery men men and so on. The commuter, in a sense, brought back the wealth from the centre and spent it in the suburb, creating a satellite economy. All Victorian suburbs, from the grandest in the West End to the most threadbare lower-middle-class enclave, reflected this. They carried within them a working-class population which was always liable to lower the tone of the district and send them scuttling off elsewhere.

By 1900, not all middle-class families had fled to the farthest ends of the commuter railway line. Many quite fashionable areas remained as islands of gentility in the general sea of decline: for example parts of Hackney, Hampstead, Dulwich or Brixton. Before the arrival of the motor car, it was common for the well-to-do to live along the main roads, and the maps that the social investigator Charles Booth produced in the 1890s show this clearly. Booth had his own, colour-coded class classification which he used to shade in the social and 'moral' character of the whole of the inner part of the metropolis. All over London, the main roads are lined with the brown of his category of people second in the social scale: shopkeepers living above their premises, or middle-class families in semi-detached villas.

The West End did contain pockets of severe poverty, but the central part of it was never subject to the waves of social change which affected more modest suburbs. In the second half of the nineteenth century a distinction was becoming established between commuter traffic, and the traffic problems of the central area – which was given over more and more to commerce, offices, government buildings, shopping and entertainment.

Orchard Road, Plumstead, in 1910. By this time cheap transport meant that the tentacles of the respectable working-class suburbs, with their scrubbed doorsteps and tidy front gardens, were reaching out in all directions several miles from the old City

A brand new terrace, almost ready for occupation, in Colebrooke Road, Walthamstow, in the 1880s. These houses would probably have been rented by artisans, labourers in regular employment and lower clerks, some of whom would have commuted into the central areas

As new forms of transport developed in the nineteenth century, a pattern had been established whereby the West End was protected from invasion by the railway and the horse tram. Most commuter routes were to the City, while the horse bus and the hansom cab provided transport in the West End – the railways were regarded as too destructive to be tolerated, and the horse tram was socially unacceptable. The cutting of the first Underground railway, the Metropolitan, and its extension around London's core with the building of the Circle Line, did not radically alter the situation. A passenger could travel from Euston to Victoria on the Circle, but it was a long and sooty way round. Remarkably, this age of steam on the London Underground can still be recalled. George Spiller remembers working on the footplate in the first years of this century:

> We worked ten-hour days, eight times round the Circle. Then we used to run out into the open, perhaps do three Wimbledons a day, or three Ealings, or Upminster – that was the longest one – took nearly half a day to get there from the other side. It was all right when we got out into the open, but there were a lot of tunnels we had to go through first. In the summer you could hardly breathe going through the tunnels, it was so hot. It was enough to boil you

on the footplate. You took your jacket off and stripped down to your shirt. There was a terrific wind and smoke going through the tunnels, then sometimes we had rotten coal and we used to get smoked out on the footplate, but that didn't happen very often. I'd shovel about two hundredweight in a day's work: it was a dirty, hot, sweaty job, but we had to put up with it. And there was no cover outside. So we had to put up with the rain and the wind and the snow.

But this type of travel, and the impenetrability of the central areas, was transformed by the discovery of deep tunnelling methods in the late nineteenth century. In 1890, the first Underground using this method burrowed all the way from King William Street in the City to Stockwell. It was now possible to criss-cross London without destroying buildings or upsetting the carriages and sensibilities of the upper crust. The Central Line, connecting the West End and the City, was opened in 1900, and the whole of the Underground system in central London – with the exception of the Victoria and Jubilee Lines – was established in the few years of the Edwardian era. The successful electrification of railway lines was essential for the deep new Underground system, while above ground electric power replaced horse power on the trams in the first years of this century.

With the development of the Underground, the old pattern of transport in London came to an end: trains ran right through the centre, opening up the West End for office building in the 1920s and gradually undermining its exclusivity. On the buses, the petrol engine

George Spiller (centre), on the footplate of a District Railway locomotive in the 1900s, vividly remembers his work as a fireman in the age of steam-hauled Underground trains

An Underground poster of 1908 conjures up an idyllic image of suburban life in Golders Green, to encourage the middle class to move out to metro land

quickly replaced horse power, though horses continued to pull carts and goods wagons for another half century. For the most exclusive, the motor car replaced the carriage, again marking a new era in London's transport.

Between the two World Wars, London's built-up area was to continue to expand at a phenomenal rate. A new kind of semi-detached suburbia – metro land – was built along the Tube lines. It was the growth of this metro land that finally marked the end of the era of horse-drawn traffic.

CHAPTER FIVE

The
MAKING
of the
SUBURBS

Previous pages: *As the Victorian spec' built suburbs spread outwards from London, covering the countryside in great tides of bricks and mortar, brickfields like those (below) at Wood Street, Walthamstow in 1880 and rows of half-built house like those (above) at Prospect Hill, Walthamstow in 1892, must have been common sights in areas that we are now accustomed to think of as permanent urban fixtures on the landscape*

I T TAKES quite a leap of the imagination now to picture places like Paddington, Kensington, Islington, Camden Town, Camberwell or Acton as newly-built suburbs on the edge of town, their streets leading off into fields and market gardens. Although it is obvious that they must have been like that, and that London was not dropped in one large block on the landscape, there is an odd fascination in examining old photographs which show meadows and trees which became another suburban road in, say, Hornsey or Muswell Hill. An imaginative reconstruction of the way in which the countryside around London became built up does help to explain why places which are now part of the 'inner city' – a term which is a by-word for urban desolation – were once thought of as suburbs. Whatever else 'suburban' means, it has always been a term to describe the residential border areas between town and country.

But to imagine Victorian suburbs were simply an older version of the places which go by that name today is misleading. The suburban 'ideal' of a house away from the noise and bustle of the centre of town may

The bridge from Middle Lane to Priory Road, Hornsey, in the 1860s. At this time Hornsey was still little more than a village, surrounded by hay fields and market gardens, beyond the suburban sprawl

not have been very different, but the physical reality of Victorian suburbia was in many ways another world. Even the most salubrious new developments in Kensington or Paddington contained in stinking enclaves terrible slums. Until late in the nineteenth century, most suburbs had defective sewage systems, the roads were liberally spread with the manure of horse-drawn vehicles, and for all their comparative grandness they could never have achieved the scrubbed primness of later, semi-detached suburbia.

In fact, the more the word 'suburbia' is examined, the more puzzling it becomes. Over the centuries it has been used to describe just about every condition of town life imaginable. In Elizabethan times it referred to the miserable settlements of outcasts and poor immigrants who couldn't find a place in town. It has been applied to the habit of wealthier merchants and financiers from the City setting themselves up in country villas way beyond the urban frontier in the late eighteenth and early nineteenth centuries. And much later in the nineteenth century, when artisans and poorer clerks could afford to live in places like Tottenham and Walthamstow, we hear of 'working-class' suburbs. What is there left of London which was never 'suburban' at one time or another? Very little.

The truth is that London is a metropolis of suburbs and really has been so since the seventeenth century. Whereas most European cities, such as Paris, developed within a clearly defined boundary marked by defensive walls, London began to spread out from the square mile of the City very early on. And from the very earliest developments a distinctive pattern of building was established which remained characteristic of London and the English until suburbia became a common form of townscape throughout the world in the twentieth century.

It has always amused foreigners that Londoners liked to live in separate houses rather than flats. A Frenchman remarked in 1817: 'These narrow houses, three or four storeys high . . . one for eating, one for sleeping, a third for company, a fourth underground for the kitchen, a fifth perhaps at the top for the servants . . . and the agility, the ease, the quickness with which the individuals of the family run up and down, and perch on the different storeys, give the idea of the cage with its sticks and its birds.'

On the other hand, the more pompous English Victorians thought the French upper crust very peculiar because they did not mind living in the same block as their social inferiors. An article in the magazine *Architecture* commented in the 1870s:

It would be difficult to quote any custom of the French which English people might less readily fall in with than that which assigns the tenancy of the half dozen successive storeys of the same house to just as many utterly dissociated and indeed discordant people, ranging from a jaunty viscount of the *premier étage*, not merely to a very small rentier on the *troisième*, but to a little nest of the humblest work people on the *cinquième*, all meeting on the common stair. . .

Why well-to-do Londoners should have developed a taste for individual houses rather than apartments is not at all clear, but it had important consequences for the way in which suburbia developed. The desire to live away from the workplace, and the centre of town, was never simply the result of taste for a semi-rural kind of existence as has often been suggested. It always seems to have had more to do with establishing one's superior social status, and other practical and quite unromantic considerations. For example, was a banker who set himself up in a 'country' villa in Dulwich in the early 1800s seeking rural tranquillity or a lifestyle which mimicked that of the landed gentry? Was the clerk who settled in a house in Islington or Camberwell really trying to experience a semi-rural existence, or was he simply fulfilling his ideal of living in a house of his own, and these were the only places sufficiently near work that he could afford to rent? It is really impossible to answer such questions, but a good deal of writing on suburbia seems to assume that it was semi-ruralness that provided the essential appeal, and that the back garden is the suburbanite's imaginary field and hedgerow. Whatever truth there is in the idea, it should not obscure the much more serious business of suburbia, which involved establishing one's class position and finding a house in which one could afford to live.

One illustration of this aspiration towards social superiority was the common and characteristically lower-middle-class habit of christening a small terraced house or villa with a grandiose and pretentious name. William Head for example, brought up in Stafford Road, Hounslow in the 1900s, remembers, 'We lived in a villa with a lovely bay window which my father bought for £250. The house was designated Longleat Villa, I suppose to be a spot above the rest of the neighbours and to keep up our connection with Wiltshire where Father came from.'

Moreover the idyllic portraits of Victorian suburbia which sometimes appear in contemporary advertisements and nostalgic middle-class memoirs, should not be allowed to mask the fact that what made most comfortable suburban homes tick was the regimented and unremitting toil of low paid domestics. Ronald Chamberlain whose father worked as a post office clerk in the City, was brought up in Canonbury in the early part of this century. He remembers how the young domestics employed by the family would occasionally desert their duties when it all became too much for them.

> In our home we always had a little maid of all work, of about fourteen or fifteen, who had to work hard all day. The little girl would bring in her alarm clock to be wound and my father would set it for half past six, when she would be expected to get up sharp.

The erection of Leyton Hall, Goldsmith Road, in 1912. Building suburbia was a major London industry employing tens of thousands – bricklayers, master builders, surveyors and so on

A maid buys wild strawberries from a young street trader in 1877. It was the hidden 'maid of all work' whose lowly paid labour made most suburban homes tick

She'd have her meals by herself in the kitchen and would go to bed about half past nine. On more than one occasion these little girls would run away and go home, they couldn't stand it any more.

Although suburbia was based on the ideal of an individual home of one's own the great mass of detached and semi-detached villas and terraces that were put up in the eighteenth and nineteenth centuries were not custom built for particular clients. Few people had the luxury of ordering a particular style of house: popular taste was established in the market place by estate owners and speculative builders. Land around London was plentiful and cheap and most of it was suitable for building, or could be made suitable once the art of drainage had been developed. It was therefore sensible to put up relatively simple, individual structures with a low density of population. And as the demand for housing grew with the great increase in population, it was inevitable that London would simply spread outwards. Those who were supplying the house may therefore have been as influential as those renting them in shaping the suburban character of the capital.

House building and the creation of suburbia was a major London industry. It required capital from the City, and in fact drew in funds from all over the country. For the landowner it was a way of raising ground rents way above those provided by market gardeners or farmers. It provided work for professional surveyors and solicitors, who not only handled the legal work but were commonly responsible for raising money for speculative builders. The speculative builders themselves, from the giants like Thomas Cubitt to the mass of smaller 'master builders' or craftsmen, could make a fortune, though they more frequently went bankrupt. And the building industry employed tens of thousands of labourers, as well as all those involved in supplying essential materials such as bricks.

On the ground, the ideal of suburbia was a very serious business. For the most part, the owners of the large country estates surrounding London in the eighteenth century – many of which still exist as valuable town properties today – were anxious that when their land became ripe for development it should become as fashionable a part of town as possible. On the other hand, they were not usually prepared to take the risk involved in putting up houses themselves. What they preferred to do was to grant a building lease to a speculative builder, and though they might lend him some money towards the cost of putting up houses, he took the gamble on whether or not they would be let. In the short term, the estate received increased ground rents from the property: in the long term, the entire development would come back into its ownership when the lease expired, and the wealthier the tenants the more valuable the estate in the future. Good estate management, therefore, involved ensuring the 'right' sort of houses were built to attract the 'right' sort of people.

The owners of land north of Westminster and west of the City had a head start in the eighteenth century. Proximity to the royal palaces and Parliament was obviously a good selling point if you wanted to attract the aristocracy and gentry. The fact that the Grosvenor estate, for example, owned large unbroken tracts of land made planned development relatively easy on a large scale. The Duke of Bedford's estate, north of the Strand, was similarly well placed to provide new housing for both the titled Londoners who had a country estate, and the wealthy merchants of the City who, since the Great Fire, sought a home outside the old square mile.

But building was always a gamble: if, for some reason, the housing you put up did not attract the clientele you were aiming for, the estate could quickly go down hill. It was not thought sufficient simply to build large, elegant houses – the supply of these was constantly being renewed by developers elsewhere, seeking the same kind of tenant. You had to do what you could to keep out the sort of people who might make the estate unattractive. In the 1850s, the leases on the Bedford estate prohibited an astonishing array of tradesmen from occupying its buildings: 'Brewer, slaughterer, distiller, dyer, goldbeater, tanner, bone boilers, soapboilers, working hatter. . . .' These, and many more activities were banned.

Agents advertise a family residence to let in Beckenham in the 1900s. Building was always a gamble and if properties didn't attract the 'right' sort of clientele or any clientele at all, then builders were faced with bankruptcy. The 'To be let' sign illustrates how most families, even middle-class ones, would rent rather than buy homes

In addition, the Bedford estate, and many other Georgian developments, put up gates to keep undesirables out of the squares and streets occupied by the wealthiest tenants, and to keep down the noise: an early example of what modern local authority planning in a more democratic way has tried to do in 'environmental areas' by cutting out through traffic from residential streets. On the Bedford estate, the gate-keepers were instructed to allow in only gentlemen on horseback and carriages, as well as pedestrians. Droves of cattle, omnibuses, carts and other 'low vehicles' were kept out. And the gates were closed at night. In 1879, people protesting about the inconvenience to normal traffic caused by such gates estimated that there were about one hundred and fifty in London.

The sort of people and traffic the estate tried to exclude gives an indication of the enormous range of essential activities that took place in nineteenth-century London, but were always being pushed into some corner and hidden away. Where did the cow-keepers, chimney sweeps, tripe-sellers, poulterers, die-sinkers, and dealers in old iron go? Or live? Most of them had to stay near their work, which was closely linked to the fashionable places from which they were excluded. So, they ended up in appalling slums, jam-packed into tiny back alleys, disused stables, and buildings that for one reason or another had fallen into disrepair. On the Bedford estate, some shoddily built housing in Abbey Place became a slum, and there were no grand housing developments anywhere that did not develop their hideous slum quarters.

Paradise Row, Agar Town, a notorious shanty town slum in the mid-nineteenth century. Estate managers lived in fear that pockets of poverty like this would drag down the social tone of an entire estate, thus spelling financial disaster for the owners. There was no thought of providing housing for the poorer classes, on whose labour the building and servicing of these estates depended

Away from the estates, on the fringes of the built-up area, Victorian shanty towns developed. Not far from Bedford Square, just to the north on the other side of the New Road was Agar Town. In a technical and legal sense, this had been built in the same way as Bedford Square: the Church Commissioners leased the land to a developer, a lawyer called William Agar. But Agar did not insist on a high standard of building, or strict leasing arrangements when he brought in cheap labour – bricklayers and carpenters working in their spare time – to put up the streets of houses. Agar Town became an instant slum, which was described by Charles Dickens in 1851 in the magazine, *Household Words*:

> Along the canal side the huts of the settlers, of many shapes and sizes, were closely ranged, every tenant having his own lease of the ground. There the dog-kennel, the cow shed, the shanty, and the elongated match-box style of architecture. . . Through an opening was to be seen another layer of dwellings at the back: one looking like a dismantled windmill, and another perched upon a wall. . . Every garden had its nuisance. . . . In the one was a dung-heap, in the next a cinder-heap, in a third, which belonged to the cottage of a costermonger, was a pile of whelk and periwinkle shells, some rotten cabbages, and a donkey.

The contrast between the heavily fortified elegance of Bedford Square and the squalour of Agar Town is a classic example of the extreme range of wealth and social conditions to be found in Victorian London. And it was often argued at the time that the policy of the estates in keeping out undesirables, and not providing the lowest class with any housing, was the cause of the slum problem. But others, looking back on the careful way in which the estates were controlled, have held them up as models of town planning, which was abandoned in the building of the Victorian suburbs.

However, there was always tremendous social tension in suburb building, and though estate management undoubtedly became much less rigorous as the nineteenth century wore on, the same battle to create a fashionable area – whether it was to appeal to the upper classes or the lower middle classes – was played out in Hampstead, Islington, Acton, Ealing, Camberwell, Hackney, Peckham and just about everywhere except the lost tracts of the East End of London.

It is arguable that the Georgian estates, like the Bedford development, were not true suburbs in the sense that they were really extensions of London's centre, and built in an urban rather than suburban fashion. It could also be said that places like Agar Town, shoddily built on land blighted by the new railway yards carved out of the fringes of London, were not truly suburbs because they had such a low social character. The suburb proper was middle class and essentially tied in with the habit of commuting into town to work, by foot, horse bus or train. It all depends, of course, on what you classify as suburban. Do you include the scatter of detached and semi-detached villas that were built in the countryside around London in the early nineteenth century, as well as the isolated terrace rows that sprang up in places like Camberwell, Stockwell, Canonbury, Stoke Newington and Hackney? They were suburban in the sense that they provided semi-rural homes for those linked socially and economically to the centre of town.

There were other forms of suburban development, too, which do not quite fit the classic image of suburbia. Squares and streets of terraced houses were built to form small-scale urban centres on the outskirts of the City and the West End. They were often called 'towns' and bits of them remain as a kind of nucleus around which much more extensive suburbia took place: Camden Town, Kentish Town, Kensington New Town, or De Beauvoir Town. There were some built to the east of the City – Tredegar Square or Bromley New Town, for example – before the East End took on its later nineteenth-century character.

The villas with their parkland (now built over, or turned into municipal parks, such as Marble Hill in Twickenham or Clissold Park in Hackney) and the new towns obviously embodied a kind of suburban ideal, but at the time they were built they really remained distant from the social forces that were shaping the greater London which grew out to engulf them. For the most part their *distance* from the centre would ensure their relative exclusivity at least for a time, whereas the inner London estates had to create an artificial remoteness.

On the whole, however, nineteenth-century suburbia had neither gates nor distance to protect it from the ever-present threat of social decline. Its development was much less carefully controlled than the West End estates: it took shape and found its social level in a gingerly, and not always predictable, way. As less grand landlords and smaller builders copied in miniature and caricatured earlier villa and terrace styles for tenants who had more social pretension than money, so suburbs often took on a characteristic stamp of mass-produced and often hang-dog gentility.

No two suburbs developed in quite the same way, because the intricacies of the land dealings and speculations, together with the foibles of builders, ensured an odd mixture of individuality within the general conformity. And though we tend to imagine suburbs as clearly defined places, their boundaries were never very clear, just as the districts of London today – Clapham, Highbury, Chelsea, Kensington or Hampstead – really have no identifiable borders. The names of areas and streets reflected a host of influences: the titles of landowners, the original names of villages, builders' names, and often some obscure references to members of their families.

You can find, for example, in Brixton – today regarded as one of the saddest examples of inner-city decline – a Minet Road. It's named after the Minet family, French Huguenots who came to England in the early eighteenth century to escape religious persecution. They became bankers in the City and in Dover, and bought land in the Brixton area which remained almost entirely rural until the early 1800s. As London pushed outwards, the Minet estate, along with others in the Camberwell and Brixton areas, became ripe for development.

Typically, the first housing built on Brixton Hill and Denmark Hill was in the form of detached villas or terraces which followed the main roads. In 1826, for example, the Minets were granting building leases for a terrace called 'Surrey Villas' on Camberwell New Road. Brixton and Camberwell were then very salubrious areas, and remained fashionable with City people until early this century.

But the Minet estate was only extensively built up after the 1860s, with the opening of Loughborough Junction Station and, after 1870, with the arrival of the horse tram. This brought in a new population of clerks and some artisans, and Brixton itself developed as a local shopping area, where the Bon Marche, one of the first – though not very successful – department stores was built in 1877.

In the 1880s a guidebook, *The Suburban Homes of London*, declared the Brixton Road 'as good a specimen of a modern suburban thoroughfare as can well be met with'. And in 1889, the social class

Acre Lane, Brixton, in the 1900s. This part of Brixton, with its large villas and tree-lined roads, was considered very genteel and desirable. It attracted carriage people, City businessmen, and professional people – especially music-hall and theatre stars – some of whom could afford several servants

maps produced by Charles Booth show little poverty in this area. The Minet estate was in fact, a classic Victorian suburb, quintessentially 'genteel' according to the guidebook.

One of the best descriptions of the way in which a nineteenth-century suburb developed is given in Professor F.M.L. Thompson's history of Hampstead. The whole district derived its character from a mixture of local peculiarities, geography, its position in relation to central London, and forces which made the metropolis grow. The small town of Hampstead had been, briefly, a spa which attracted artists, and doctors amongst other professionals. In the period before the great explosion of housing that joined it to central London, villas and terraces such as Church Row were built, making Hampstead an out-of-town suburb with a professional rather than an aristocratic character. By the 1860s it had more domestic servants per household than any other district of London. What Hampstead lacked – and the West End districts of the gentry had in plenty – were footmen and other male servants associated with the very top, carriage-owning class.

Between the small town of Hampstead and Regent's Park lay a large estate owned by Eton College. This tract of land covered what is now known as Chalk Farm, as well as parts of districts called, uncertainly, Belsize Park, Swiss Cottage and Primrose Hill. In the early nineteenth century the lessee had sub-let the land to a farmer who used it as grazing land for livestock and dairy cattle. As Regent's Park took shape and St John's Wood developed into the prototype upper-middle-class suburb of villadom – it became clear that Eton College's land would be very valuable for building development.

As far as estate development was concerned, the College does not appear to have been too dynamic: it received a good rent from farming, and could increase the rate when leases expired. But in 1826 it did take the first step that all landowners required if they were to grant building leases: an Act of Parliament was obtained to abolish existing manorial rights on the land. (Hampstead Heath remained open country because the landowner, Sir Thomas Maryon Wilson, uniquely amongst would-be developers, for complex legal reasons couldn't get his Act through Parliament.)

In 1829, the Eton College surveyor offered fifteen acres of the estate for development with the recommendation: 'This very desirable property, which is too well known to render necessary any description of its eligibility in all respects for Villas and respectable residences, combining the advantages of Town and Country.' But this was not a boom period in London building and, although three hundred yards of Adelaide Road were laid out, nothing much happened – in the way of house building, that is. For in 1831 the railway chugged onto the scene.

The London & Birmingham wanted to push its line to Camden Town and Euston right through the Eton College estate. The farmer protested, the College equivocated, and a compromise was reached. The railway had to be contained in a tunnel built solidly enough to carry the house building that the estate anticipated would take place on top. In 1838 the tunnel – the first in London – was opened. As the trains emerged from the elaborately detailed entrance so they attracted sightseers, but the building speculators stayed away. There was some talk at the time of the railway 'opening up' the area for development, but this was rather absurd. The London & Birmingham was a long-distance line with no local stations until Kilburn was opened in 1852, and South Hampstead in 1879. By that time, the Eton College estate had already been developed.

With the railway – which elsewhere, in Kentish Town and Camden Town, caused almost instant blight – safely tucked in its tunnel and deep cutting, the building speculators eventually began to turn up. One grand scheme, proposed by a developer, was to put up villas like those that John Nash had built not long before in Regent's Park. But the College rejected it. In the meantime, the prime site of Primrose Hill was preserved when Eton College agreed to give it to the Crown, in return for a chunk of Crown lands near Eton.

Typically, the area then took shape over a long period as builders turned up, took parcels of land, and put up the sort of housing – such as the semi-detached villas along Adelaide Road – which they thought would attract an upper-middle-class, St John's Wood type of clientele. As new roads were cut, and new houses built it was recognized as with

Primrose Hill Tunnel on the London & North Western Railway, shortly after it was built in 1838. The Eton College Estate, who owned the land, only allowed the line to pass through it on the condition that it was contained in a tunnel built solidly enough to carry the house building that the estate anticipated would take place on top

a new council estate of the 1950s, that there were no community facilities on the estate. This worried the local builders. John Shaw, the surveyor, passed on their sentiments to the College:

> I find there is a general need for a Chapel on the estate. . . . Mr Wynn, the builder of many houses, and other persons, have led me to believe that it would be profitable even as a speculation to establish one. . . . Undoubtedly the existence of such a building on the estate would most materially lead to the formation of a neighbourhood around it.

Developers commonly regarded a church as the essential feature of a middle-class suburb, and a selling point. The other community facility was the public house – and this very often arrived sooner than the church. The Eton College estate was provided with the Adelaide Hotel in 1842 and the Eton Hotel in 1846 (both pubs), but had to wait until 1856 before St Saviour's Church was completed. By the 1870s, the estate had two churches and two pubs, representing a classically respectable middle-class area in Victorian London.

The estate's 'success' in these terms was something of a fluke because the development had never been really well planned, and the most important decision of the estate turned out to be the sinking of the railway underground. Had the rival landowner, Sir Thomas Maryon Wilson, been able to develop all his estate in the area, Eton College might well have suffered from the competition. There was no provision made for industry, which not only polluted areas but brought in a working-class population, and the people who moved in were not generally carriage-owning folk, so not many stables were built: when a mews was not used for horses, it was, of course, commonly turned into a slum.

The experience of a district not far away from Chalk Farm, and still close to Hampstead Heath, was very different, and gives a good idea why some suburban building didn't quite take off in the way intended. Land owned by the Dean and Chapter of Westminster on the Belsize estate was let out on long leases which effectively prevented the estate owners from overseeing building themselves. One of the leaseholders was William Lund, who had forty-five acres off Haverstock Hill. He decided to go in for a kind of 'St John's Wood' development, and called his estate St John's Park. It was close to the newly opened Hampstead Road Station on the North London Line, and Lund hoped that he might attract City people.

Lund lived in Haverstock Lodge, with eight acres of grounds, and set about developing the estate himself by building around his home. He surrendered his existing lease and took out a ninety-nine-year building lease which was only loosely drawn up by the Dean and Chapter of Westminster. Everything went well at first, and within ten years he had built sixty semi-detached villas. But uncontrollable elements soon set the estate on a downhill path. First, St John's Park sloped away down to the River Fleet, which had become an open sewer by the 1850s; it was not put into underground pipes until the following decade. The sewer blighted one corner of the estate. Next, a branch of the Midland Railway into St Pancras was tunnelled under the estate, creating uncertainty about its desirability amongst builders. Finally, in 1869, the Metropolitan Asylums Board took over an area of unused paddocks next to the estate and put up wooden fever wards to cope with smallpox epidemics, one of which duly broke out in 1870. This obviously did nothing to increase the attractions of the area: Lund was left with unlet houses and an exodus of residents from established parts of the estate.

In 1865, a distraught resident of Upper Park Road had written to the Dean and Chapter of Westminster about the blight on the area and the deterioration of the Fleet Road end of St John's Park: 'The older houses are already greatly deteriorated in value and will be still more so if these shops are opened as being in Upper Park Road, and after expending a large sum of money in purchasing, furnishing, and fitting up this house it will be very annoying to be driven away.'

Most of the Belsize estate did not deteriorate in this way and, in fact, the area to the east of Fleet Road did not become a slum: more the home of artisans and respectable working people. Also, significantly, while the horse trams were kept out of Hampstead as a whole, as they were from other middle-class areas, they arrived in Fleet Road and South End Green in the 1870s to put the final lower-middle-class and working-class stamp on this fringe part of Hampstead.

As the building of suburbia continued throughout the Victorian and Edwardian eras, so the same kinds of influences shaped the social character of districts everywhere. Railways which linked a far-flung village with London and helped it to become a salubrious suburb, blighted districts along the route. Unattractive elements – such as a lunatic asylum, a cemetery or an established industry – branded the future development of large areas.

In west London, for example, Turnham Green and Ealing developed as middle-class suburbs, while Hanwell, Acton and Brentford never provided the necessary attraction. Although short stage-coaches and horse buses linked Turnham Green and Ealing with the City in the 1830s, there was not a great deal of house building at this period. It was not until the 1850s that a continuous line of housing took shape along the principal roads leading from Notting Hill, Hammersmith and Turnham Green to Brentford. Gunnersbury Park, once a royal residence, and bought by the Rothschilds in 1835, was one of a number of earlier, remote and semi-rural out-of-town developments.

The fate of Hanwell was sealed early on when a large lunatic asylum was built to the west. In 1854, moreover, Kensington and St George's Westminster, decided to bury their dead in the same area, creating large cemeteries. Around the same time, a Central London District school for a thousand Poor Law pupils was established in the area. Such was the stigma attached to these developments that attempts were made to get Hanwell's name changed, but without success.

In Acton, where a large estate was developed by the British Land Company, the housing does not seem to have attracted a sufficient body of middle-class people to protect the area from poorer tradespeople. In 1872, there were sixty laundries – an essential Victorian service provided by women with a reputation for heavy drinking which shocked respectable middle-class opinion – on the Land Company's South Acton estate, as well as slaughter houses, and factories for the manufacture of manure from bone crushing.

Brentford, an urban area rather than a demure residential village when the great suburban expansion took off after 1860, was similarly marked out as less salubrious than Ealing or Turnham Green. It was a centre of the brewing industry, and had a soap factory and gas works.

The Notting Dale Piggeries in North Kensington in the 1860s. Many of the predominantly Irish inhabitants settled here after being evicted from their slum dwellings, razed to make way for new roads and railways. They eked out a subsistence living from pig-keeping, brick-making, street-selling and, particularly important amongst the women, laundry work. This sort of shanty town slum lowered the tone of adjoining suburbs and made them less desirable for the well-to-do

Another reason that some estates did not 'make it' in the fierce competition to attract wealthy, or at least respectable, people was a failure of the development at some stage before it was finished, leaving houses without roofs, or windows. This would prove useless to the rich but very attractive to the poor who were being pushed out of central London by clearances for new roads, railways and office building. North Kensington developed in this way when ambitious builders went bankrupt.

It seems also to have been at least one of the reasons why one of the worst slums in London was created in Campbell Road, Finsbury Park,

built in the 1860s. Freeholders on the Seven Sisters estate decided to cash in on the North Islington housing boom of the 1850s by selling off individual plots for house building on a new street running north from Seven Sisters Road. This policy of selling off to builders plot by plot – rather than any attempt to orchestrate a continuous development – left gaps between houses, and unfinished shells. The houses themselves appear not to have been any worse than the average, three-storeyed, flat-fronted buildings that were put up in their thousands all over London. Moreover, they did attract the lower middle classes – this wasn't, after all, far from Charles Pooter's fictitious home, *The Laurels*, Brickfield Terrace. In 1871 there were some residents with servants: an accountant, a barrister's clerk and a law stationer. But the incomplete state of the road, described later by a local vicar as 'unfinished, unpaved, unmade and unlighted . . . little better than an open sewer' made it less desirable, led to reduced rents and allowed in coal porters, charwomen, shoe-blacks and chimney sweeps.

Very soon, the houses intended for single occupation were being turned into lodging houses and tenements. In 1888 three of the houses were sold to one of the thousands of London landlords who made a good living by packing families into single rooms and getting a return on their property by creating overcrowding. By 1900 Campbell Road was one of the most notorious slums in London.

But for the most part these great tracts of Victorian suburbia did not go into instant decline. The very poorest people were crammed into pockets of appalling housing, while the majority of working-class and lower-middle-class Londoners found, by the standards of the time, a reasonable house somewhere. It should be remembered that inside toilets and bathrooms were very rare features, even in better households, until quite late in the nineteenth century.

Hackney, perhaps, provides as good an example as any of the standard London suburb of the period. No more than a village at the start of the nineteenth century, it began to become a part of London in the 1850s. It had its typical, out-rider development of De Beauvoir Town – laid out in the 1830s and 1840s in a grid pattern in a modest version of a grander estate in town. In 1851, the *Illustrated London News* reported that W.G.D. Tyssen, the descendant of a Flemish merchant, had begun to lay out his land for building development. The railway had just arrived – again the North London Line – always a spur to building, though the horse omnibus had linked Hackney with central London from the 1840s.

Typically, small-scale building speculators put up the semi-detached villas and terraces designed to cater for the tastes of City people. Often a builder would be responsible for only one house in the street, and few operated on a large enough scale to build more than half a dozen houses. Thus the variations on the theme of villa and terrace – with architectural style and detail gleaned from the many handbooks available – took shape.

In Hackney, housing was graded to some extent and, where a middle-class family might not be attracted, smaller, lower-grade terraces were provided for the working classes. Dalston Lane in the 1860s housed a number of clerks, as well as master craftsmen, printers and commercial travellers, in three- and four-bedroomed terraced properties with steps up to the front door. Leading off this main road were poorer streets, where labourers, boot-makers and plasterers lived.

Parts of Hackney would never make it as a 'clerk's paradise': Homerton, for example, had a smallpox hospital and two workhouses, all established before suburban development began; Hackney Wick, meanwhile, was too near the industries of the Lea Valley. But, by and large, Hackney became well established as a desirable middle- and lower-middle-class suburb, and remained so until the end of the century.

In the long run, however, Hackney was in the wrong part of London to retain its social pretensions. As the East End developed, so it began to encroach on, and to surround, a suburb which had been built close to open country and away from industry. Cheap workmens' fares

A bay-windowed terrace aimed at a lower-middle-class market, nearing completion in the Clapton district of Hackney in the 1880s. But by the beginning of the Great War, clerks and managers had moved out of Hackney to escape from the newly mobile working class who had begun to colonize the entire area

Upper Hornsey Rise, complete with toll gates, in the 1860s, when it lay on the edge of the countryside. By the eve of the First World War it had become firmly locked into London's suburban sprawl

introduced on the Great Eastern Railway allowed a new section of the trapped central population of London to move out to places north and east of Hackney, where speculators put up a meaner form of housing to cater for a new kind of clientele. And industry, pushed out of the City and kept away from the fashionable West End, moved towards Hackney, until it was almost incorporated into the East End.

Hackney declined as a well-heeled suburb because it found on its doorstep not just socially undesirable working-class folk but, even worse, the criminal classes who increasingly made Hoxton, on its south-western outskirts, their home. As Ted Harrison, the son of a Hoxton street sweeper, recalls, the 'dangerous classes' – poor people who defied the law – found rich pickings in areas like De Beauvoir. Even children joined in this harassment of the propertied, waging a war against their better-off peers.

> One reason that the posher people who used to live in Hackney moved out, the managers of department stores, foremen, people like that, was because they didn't like living so close to us lot in Hoxton. It was a common saying 'if you put a net around Hoxton you'd have half the criminals of the world'. They'd do a bit of house-breaking in places where people could afford to lose it, like De Beauvoir. If we

saw a college boy, we'd snatch his hat off and fill it up with horse shit, then give it to him back. We were rotten when we went into the posher areas, we wouldn't do it in our own street. When the police tried to arrest anybody they'd have to come in pairs, and there was a riot then because people used to get onto the roofs and chuck stuff down at them.

An extraordinary picture of the social structure of London, after a century of unprecedented growth, is provided by the maps drawn up by the social investigator, Charles Booth. His classification of social classes is quaint: it goes from the 'vicious and semi-criminal', marked in black, to the very wealthy, marked bright yellow, almost gold. (A detail from Booth's map of Westminster is shown on the back cover of this book.) The maps are not easy to interpret because you can never be quite sure how Booth is defining these groups: he was a great moralist, and much of his gigantic work is about the parlous state of church-going in London. But they do provide at a glance a picture of how variegated the social picture had become. Some areas in the West End are mostly bright yellow; some in south London and the East End show the duller colours of poverty or shabby gentility. Overall, London produces a patchwork effect, with the dark blue of the slum glaring out from areas of pink and pale blue.

What the social shadings represent is a myriad of legal, economic, geographical, political and other influences which came to shape the districts of inner London. It's the story of the creation of a kind of suburban ideal by market forces which never amounted to planning in the modern sense; which often went wrong from the developer's point of view; and which created, at the height of the Empire, a capital city of terraces and villas quite distinct from anything to be found in Europe.

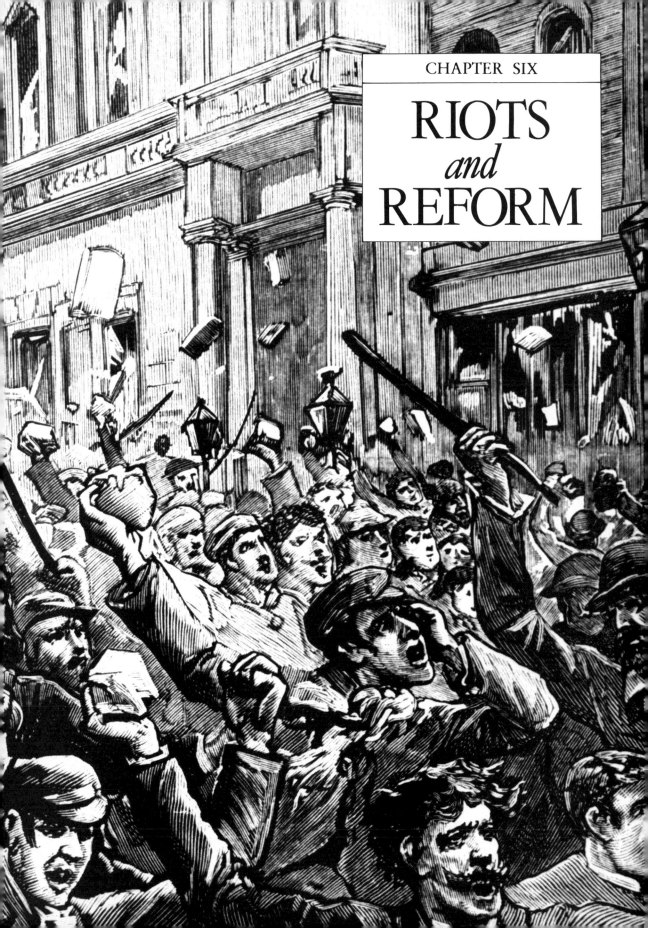

CHAPTER SIX

RIOTS
and
REFORM

FROM TIME to time an outbreak of violent crime or public disorder in London, whether real or lent lurid credibility by the popular press, gives rise to a fear that the social problems of the vast inner city will destroy its normal, workaday calm. In the past few years there have been continuous scares about street robbery, for which the term 'mugging' was resurrected, and reports that the streets of London are no longer safe. In 1981 the youth riots in Brixton, which in a few days of arson and looting destroyed a sizeable amount of property in a run-down London borough, aroused a widespread fear of the collapse of law and order in the capital. Whatever the reality of the capital's stability, the Victorian heart of London has become associated with serious problems of inadequate housing, poverty and racial tension. As in most comparisons between the present and past, there is a tendency to believe that things are getting worse; that a great city, which once hummed along harmoniously, is disintegrating under new social and economic pressures.

Yet London in the nineteenth century was undoubtedly more violent than it is today. There were occasions when its wealthier citizens feared that the great mass of the poor, whose lives and sufferings might surface from time to time, were about to rise up and destroy the city in revolution. There were many parliamentary committees which enquired into the social conditions of working-class Londoners; there were countless descriptions by medical officers of health of the appalling conditions in which the poor lived; and, bit by bit, there was social reform which took effect. It was gradually recognized that a vast metropolis could not cope with its administration by leaving it to a bundle of charities and antiquated authorities who were unable to do more than tackle its problems piecemeal. But, throughout most of the nineteenth century, there was no widespread awareness amongst the propertied and the powerful of the fact that the growth of the metropolis, the speculative housing system, the destruction of slums to build new roads and allow in railways, the creation of the East End, the undermining of traditional industries and the rise of sweated and casual labour, had contributed to generate a kind of urban desolation on a scale never before known.

Previous pages: 8 February 1886: 'The mob' – most of them poor and unemployed labourers from the East End – take their revenge on the wealthy West End as they smash club windows in St James's Street. The rich feared that London was on the verge of a revolution

Left: *A demonstration of dockers demanding wages of sixpence an hour in 1889: part of the celebrated and successful 1889 dock strike. The dockers' strike fund was boosted by donations from the Victorian Establishment – the Queen herself and the City – who welcomed this sort of orderly and organized protest as far more manageable than the mob, who had terrified them with the threat of barricades and bloodshed on the streets*

But in 1886, the complacency of the fashionable West End appeared for a few days to be directly threatened by what was referred to as 'the mob'. On Monday, 8 February, during a bitterly cold winter which had put many Londoners in the building trades and the docks out of work, a demonstration was organized in Trafalgar Square. A crowd of about twenty thousand, many of them reportedly dockers and building workers from the suburbs, turned up. *The Times* reported that: 'Their numbers were increased by a very great many of the idle class – of that large body in London who are spoken of by workers themselves as the class who want no work to do.'

The demonstrators demanded employment and were addressed with

Unemployed dockers read political graffiti scrawled onto the West India Dock gates in February 1886: 'Wanted 100,000 rioters for West End'. Irregular work, subsistence wages and grinding poverty, which were particularly rife in the East End, were the main causes of that year's revolt

revolutionary rhetoric by Ben Tillett, the dockers' leader, and John Burns from the Social Democratic Federation, a militant socialist group. An attempt was made to wind up the demonstration in an orderly fashion, but a breakaway group headed for Pall Mall. Stones were thrown at the Carlton Club windows, and several were broken. Nobody is quite sure what happened. But one witness, the Socialist Henry Hyndman, later acquitted at the Old Bailey for his part in the riot, said that the Reform Club staff had thrown nailbrushes and shoes at the demonstrators. In retaliation, the windows of a number of clubs were broken with cobble stones picked up from St James's Street, which was being repaired.

The angry crowd continued to Hyde Park, smashing windows of fashionable shops, and turning over the carriages, in one case stripping the coachman of his livery and taking his place on the box. Big West End stores like Marshall & Snelgrove and Peter Robinson also suffered broken windows. The demonstrators marched home with their pickings from the West End singing 'Rule Britannia', but the fear of the mob did not lift for several days.

W.H. Smith, founder of the bookshop chain and then a Member of Parliament, told the Commons that it was 'almost incredible that, for at least an hour, the most frequented streets in the West End of London should be entirely at the mercy of the mob'. His sentiments were

THE MORNING POST, WEDNESDAY, FEBRUARY 10, 1886.

D AND BURMA.

legram has been received at the

४ VICEROY, FEB. 9.
feara, who was wounded severely
gan, on the 2d of January last,
so are Simpson, Lloyd, Gwynne,

THE RIOTING IN LONDON.

FROM OUR OWN CORRESPONDENTS.

PARIS, FEB. 9.
This morning's *Matin*, *Galignani*, and *Morning News* were almost the only papers which had full particulars regarding yesterday's demonstrations in London. To-day the vendors of papers cry " La Commune à Londres," " La Grande revolution à Londres." I understand that the leaders of the met and have resolved to dmiration for the action of . It is reported that to- will contain an important . The most exaggerated culated this evening, and are telegraphing for precise

BERLIN, FEB. 9.
the Wilhelmstrasse received despatch from the German giving precise particulars utrageous scenes in the prin- he news of this Socialistic monstration, accomplished y, has produced the most this evening's papers, re- return of Mr. Gladstone riumph of the Liberals and es with the terrible foreign tions. Notwithstanding the nce of Lord Rosebery at the the European concert is titude of Greece and Servia we are again on the eve of nternal situation, Mr. Glad- Radical Government amid England.

VIENNA, FEB. 9.
ers publish full particulars

THE RIOTING IN THE WEST-END.

MORE DISTURBANCES IN TRAFAL-GAR-SQUARE.

ENCOUNTERS WITH THE POLICE.

A SURVEY OF THE DESTRUCTION.

" King Mob" may be said to have held sway in the West-end of the town on Monday evening. Panic reigned supreme there throughout the better part of yesterday. The appearance of the principal streets was such as not even the oldest inhabitant can remember. Closely-drawn shutters, barred doors, in some cases even barricades at the windows, were everywhere to be seen, and every hour or so came rumours that fresh collections of rioters were on the way. The timidity of wealth, of which economists have often preached, was forcibly illustrated, and even the suspicion of danger was sufficient to induce the shopkeepers to close their establishments and to secure their valuables with as much care as if an invading army was expected to march through the streets of the English capital. Nor were all these fears altogether groundless, for a villanous-looking crowd early commenced to assemble in Trafalgar-square, and the supine-ness of the police encouraged them to

TO THE EDITOR OF THE TIMES.

Sir,—I was proceeding this afternoon down Piccadilly alone in my carriage, when I encountered a portion of the mob returning from Trafalgar-square. My coachman at once broke into a walk and took the inside of the road, when I was suddenly assailed by four or five rough-looking, but well-dressed and well-fed young men, who smashed the windows with their fists, tore off and carried away the lamps, tried to pull the coachman, an elderly man, off the box, assaulted me, and cut my face and broke my eye-glasses. I am not aware what I have done to, or in what way I am responsible for the condition of, the workmen, whom I have often assisted and employed to do work at a high price, too often done in so unsatis-factory a manner as to require to be done over again.

I am a subscriber to various charities and hospitals, which I shall discontinue. I have always advocated the cause of the people. I shall do so no more. When I tell you I am nearly 70 years of age, you will perhaps think that my gray hairs would have protected me from such ruffianly treatment. But the British ruffian is no respecter of age or sex. I hear they even attacked ladies. If he thinks he will advance his cause or excite sympathy by such unmanly conduct, I think he will find himself mis-taken ; and it is to be hoped that the agitators or inciters to outrage—the real ruffians—will meet the punishment they so richly deserve, here or hereafter.

I am, Sir, your obedient servant,

February 8

shared by many others. A dense fog descended on London and, frightened of a repetition of the disorder, shopkeepers and some householders shuttered their windows. Wild rumours spread of a vast army coming out of the East to attack the West. Then the fog lifted, and with it the fear that London would be overturned by the down-trodden mass of its labouring classes. The crowd had never held any real threat of revolution, but the complacency of the West End had been shaken.

In fact, it now seems astonishing how those in power were willing to risk a mass revolt of the capital's working class rather than make concessions. For all the conditions were there for revolt: dreadful poverty, once highly skilled artisans reduced to 'sweated', lowly-paid labourers, and radical movements led by disenchanted workers whose interests were utterly opposed to those in power. But the revolutionary threat was for the most part restricted to the plots of a small group of radicals, and the recurrent nightmare shared by Parliament and London's wealthiest citizens of 'the mob' sacking the West End never became reality. When, painfully slowly, the government of the capital was reformed, the threat of revolution was only one of an extraordinary mixture of Victorian impulses that brought about change. In fact, one of the most important reasons why London lagged behind many other cities in tackling problems of poverty, disease and slum dwellings in the early part of the century, was because the City of London jealously guarded its power and independence. While it did not want to take on responsibility for the metropolis that had grown around it, at the same time it put up fierce resistance to any proposals in Parliament to make the new and greater London self-governing.

'The Voice of the Turtle', a cartoon from Punch, *October 1882, satirizing the way the old City of London jealously guarded its power and independence – in this case against attempts by the Liberal Government to create a more efficient local government system for the metropolis*

The City of London itself had had for a long time a highly developed, though not necessarily very efficient, system of local government. But by 1800 only a tenth of the people of what might be called greater London lived in the old square mile. Every other district of the capital had to make do with essentially rural parish vestries, quite unsuitable for the urban areas they now controlled. Moreover, many services which we now take for granted as public utilities were provided by private companies or small, *ad hoc* authorities set up for a specific purpose. All water was supplied on a commercial basis; the oldest and largest of the companies was the New River Company, founded in the early seventeenth century, with its headquarters in Islington, where there are now large Thames Water Authority offices. Water from wells and rivers – including the Thames itself – was sold in a haphazard sort of way, and right through the nineteenth century many Londoners had to walk to standpipes which were turned on for only a few hours a day. Paving and lighting were often the responsibility of a bunch of local worthies who might take care of only a small stretch of any street. Such bodies multiplied as London spread, creating a chaotic administrative tangle.

There were eight Commissioners of Sewers covering London outside the City, but by all accounts they were hopelessly inefficient. They neither insisted on proper sewage being provided in new building developments, nor did they build efficient sewage systems themselves. In fact, much of London's sewage, even in the most salubrious areas, accumulated in cesspits under the houses, their contents removed by scavengers or 'night soil' workers who would trundle the refuse out in the dark hours to hideous middens or market gardens. But often the cesspits filled up and became cesslakes, impregnating the cellars of houses with filth. If such a large house were abandoned it might become inhabited by the most desperate of all London dwellers, who spent their lives in low, unlit basements with sewage seeping through the walls.

At the same time as the sanitary condition of London was becoming steadily worse, and the Thames filthier, another social problem – crime and disorder – posed a more immediate threat to the capital. In the early 1800s there were highwaymen on the main roads into London, operating in the countryside that was later to become suburbia. For example on Hounslow Heath the carriages of the rich were held up as they travelled along the Great West Road to Bath. In the City itself a notorious gang would hang around on the eastern outskirts and drive a bullock along the streets in front of them until it was so maddened that it would smash open the boarded shop fronts so that they could be looted. Nimble-fingered young pickpockets frequented markets and crowded thoroughfares: their favourite ploy was shoot flying – gold watch chain snatching from rich gentlemen. Countless footpads as well

Garotters – the 'muggers' of the nineteenth century – at work in the dimly-lit streets of London. The immediate threat to public order posed by crime and subversive political activities led to the first major administrative reform in London – the creation of the Metropolitan Police Force in 1829

as garotters, who would throw a cord around their victim's neck and rob him – the muggers of the early nineteenth century – lurked in the streets after dark.

All that the upright citizens of London had to protect them were a rather ragged band of unpaid, and extremely reluctant, local constables and parish watchmen who were on duty only at night. There were, too, the famous Bow Street Runners, created in the eighteenth century by Henry Fielding the novelist, magistrate and reformer, and his brother. But they quickly acquired a wide reputation for tracking down criminals and stalked the country way beyond the edge of London on celebrated cases, often in the pay of wealthy gentlemen who wanted some score settled. In effect, London was very poorly policed. When there was an outbreak of civil disorder, the troops had to be called in, worsening tension and creating fear of outright conflict between people and authority.

In the Port of London itself, as we have already seen, the scale of pilfering from ships anchored and waiting to be unloaded became serious enough to threaten even the complacency of City merchants. It was on the Thames that the first proper police force was organized in 1798, signalling a major psychological change in an age when the very idea of professional policing was considered an infringement of personal liberty.

When, in the 1820s, the first proposals for a London-wide, professional force was proposed, the City of London objected violently: it would be a 'violation of all the Chartered Rights of the City'. But in this one respect, law and order, Parliament and a shrewd Home Secretary, Sir Robert Peel, were prepared to challenge the authority of the City – up to a point. A second attempt was made to establish a police force, this time allowing the City of London to have its own officers, and this was pushed through despite widespread suspicion from all classes of society.

The creation of the Metropolitan Police in 1829 was, in a sense, the first time that Parliament recognized London to be a single, indivisible metropolis. However, the police managed to create an essentially London service without setting up a local administrative body which rivalled the power of Westminster or the City. There was always a fear that if the largest city in the country were granted any kind of political autonomy, it would threaten the traditional authorities in the City and Westminster.

So that the new police force did not *look* like a military force, they were dressed up in blue uniforms with reinforced top hats, and they carried truncheons rather than swords or guns. This did not make them instantly popular, and it took some time before they managed to establish any public respect. But the Metropolitan Police had by the middle of the century become a model force, and were deployed around the country to quell disturbances.

During the 1840s they played a very important role in controlling the Chartist movement in the capital, arresting activists and breaking up public meetings. London had become one of the Chartist centres in the country, providing the movement with leaders like William Lovett and Ernest Jones, who published the most widely read Chartist newspaper, *The Northern Star*.

Amongst the Chartist demands was the vote for the working class. They often spoke in revolutionary rhetoric, believing that if poorer people had the vote they would oust the parasitic aristocracy who lived in luxury by levying taxes on the productive classes, and profiteering employers who exploited their labour. However, the Chartists were not for the most part revolutionary. And what threat they did pose was relatively easily contained by the Metropolitan Police. But the wave of revolutions in European capitals in February and March of 1848 suddenly made revolution in London seem a real possibility to those who feared it, and they took extraordinary steps to secure the capital against insurrection. The Chartist leaders announced that on Monday, 10 April there would be a mass rally on Kennington Common, followed by a march to Westminster to present the Charter containing five million signatures of working men and women from all over Britain, demanding universal suffrage.

More demonstrators arrive to swell the crowd for the famous Chartist protest meeting on Kennington Common in 1848, which among its demands wanted the vote for the working class. The authorities panicked and thousands of police, special constables and troops were drafted in to prevent the demonstrators attempting a revolution

This declaration created a panic in Parliament. It was decided that the defence of the capital could not just be left to the Metropolitan Police – although four thousand of them were to be stationed along the Thames bridges to prevent the protesters marching back to Westminster to present their petition, which the authorities feared might be the flashpoint leading to a revolution. Just about every major public building was to be guarded by 'special constables', sworn in for the occasion and armed. There is great disagreement about the number of 'specials' on duty that day, and what were the motives of the majority of those who joined up. Much newspaper comment claimed that the working classes were prepared to defend the capital by being sworn in as 'specials', but it is quite clear that a great many did so under threat of losing their jobs if they refused. A recent, carefully balanced estimate of special constables on duty on 10 April puts their numbers at eighty-five thousand.

At the same time, the Duke of Wellington, who master-minded the operation, brought in more than seven thousand soldiers, who were billeted in the West End and the City. They were kept out of sight, but were there in case of emergency. As an absolute safeguard for the monarchy, Queen Victoria left London on 8 April for Osborne House on the Isle of Wight. The most heavily fortified building was the Bank of England: sandbags were stacked along its parapet walls with loopholes for muskets and small guns, and musket batteries were set up at each corner of the building. Even the British Museum was armed with fifty muskets. One hundred cutlasses and other weapons were issued for the defence of the capital's prisons.

Quite early in the day it was recognized that all this armoury had been quite unnecessary: the demonstration was largely peaceful, and broke up without any rioting. London began to say that it had not been frightened after all and, though there were further protests and outbreaks of violence in that turbulent year, the threat of Chartism quickly faded.

It is now generally believed that the one major administrative reform in London in the first half of the nineteenth century, the creation of the police force for the whole metropolis, was an important factor in the prevention of insurrection, giving Parliament the confidence to reject out of hand Chartist demands for reform. Whether or not the political reforms that the Chartists sought would have led to a different development in London's government is a matter of conjecture. What is indisputable is that from the middle of the century onwards, the political control of the metropolis was left in the hands of Parliament and governments in Westminster, a system of local government which rapidly became outmoded as London grew in size, and vested interests – notably the City of London – who were resistant to any kind of social or political change at all. And it is worth noting that the *order* in which the great social problems of the metropolis were tackled does seem to reflect the preoccupations of those in power. The problem of crime, and the threat of disturbances, was tackled first with the creation of the Metropolitan Police in 1829. The problem of sewage was met with the setting up of the Metropolitan Board of Works in 1855. But the housing problem was left to private and philanthropic endeavour until the 1890s, though Parliament did introduce a series of more or less unsuccessful laws to encourage a solution to overcrowding and the elimination of slums.

In 1835, extensive reform of local government in England and Wales set up recognizably modern local authorities, elected by ratepayers, to tackle a host of social problems. But this Municipal Corporations Act excluded London. So too did the Town Improvements Act of 1847, which allowed local authorities outside London to involve themselves, with parliamentary approval, in drainage, water supply, street paving and so on. Parliament was simply not prepared to tread on the toes of the City of London, or the vested interests of the largely incompetent parish authorities who controlled greater London, by reforming the system of local government in the capital.

The results of neglect were so awful by the 1850s, by which time London's population had reached two and a half million that the social conditions seem almost unbelievable today. Here, for example, is a description of the water supply available to the poverty-stricken inhabitants of the notorious Jacob's Island in Bermondsey: 'In Jacob's Island may be seen at any time of the day women dipping water, with pails attached by ropes to the backs of the houses, from a foul and foetid ditch, its banks coated with a compound of mud and filth, and with offal and carrion – the water to be used for every purpose, culinary ones not excepted.'

The private, profit-making water companies had a virtual monopoly of particular areas, and often did not bother to lay on a regular supply. Invariably they found the cheapest source of water, which was often the hideously polluted Thames. In other cases, water came from wells which were shallow, filling from soil impregnated with filth. In Clerkenwell it was said that the water of the parish 'received the drainage water of Highgate cemetery, of numerous burial grounds, and of the innumerable cesspools in the district'.

A number of government investigations of the state of public health in London were instigated, some of them as a result of outbreaks of Asiatic cholera which claimed its first victims in England in 1832, and recurred sporadically in the capital. Cholera was by no means the biggest killer amongst the diseases which continually swept through the slum districts of London: 'the fever' and smallpox were to prove more deadly. But cholera had a terrible symbolic significance, though

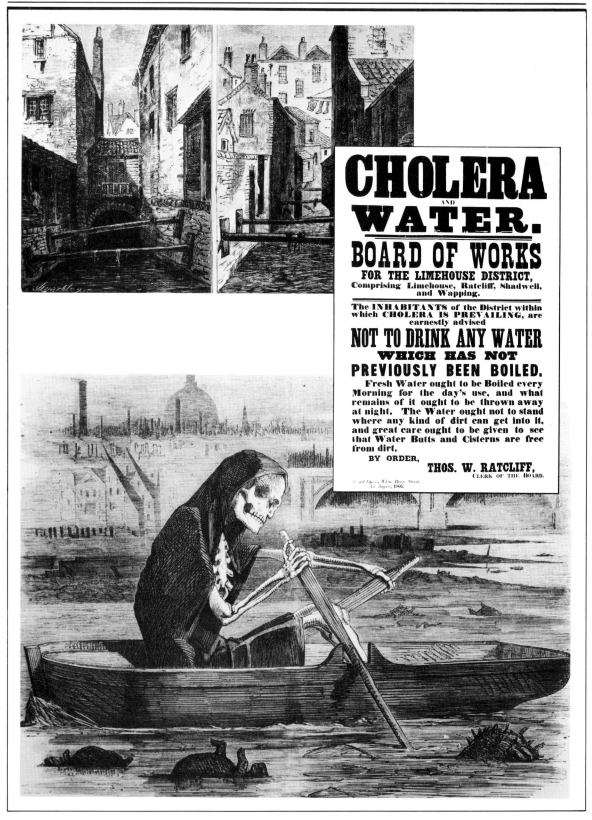

not quite terrible or threatening enough to get Parliament to act effectively. In 1847 a Royal Commission on the Health of the Metropolis led to a reform of the administration of the sewers, with new sets of commissioners under a central body, and in the previous year a General Board of Health was established, but it had few powers.

It was not until 1855, with the setting up of the Metropolitan Board of Works, that any really fundamental change was brought about in the city's sanitary condition. The Board provided London with its first, recognizable system of local government: thirty-eight new local authorities, or district boards, were established, and they along with the City of London – which remained, of course, dependent and untouched – elected the Board members. Although this marked the beginning of the end of the hopeless fragmentation of local administration in London it took a few more years – and a hot summer in which the stink of the Thames became too much for members of the House of Commons – for the Board to be given the go-ahead to solve the problem.

For two years the government and the new Board argued over the best way to create a new drainage system in London. The Board was required by law to obtain government approval for any schemes costing over £50,000, and the go-ahead from Parliament for anything over £100,000. In June 1858 rival projects and costs were still being argued over when members of the Commons Committee, including Benjamin Disraeli, were seen to make a dash from their deliberations holding handkerchiefs over their noses. The Thames, which had become more and more heavily used as a sewer, finally made its point by stinking out the Commons Committee. From then on, the Board was given a free hand to solve the problem.

In less than ten years, under their chief engineer, Sir Joseph Bazalgette, the Board completed a new main drainage system consisting of eighty-two miles of sewers, which carried a large proportion of London's effluent under the new embankment far downstream along the Thames. Gradually, the other rivers of London, such as the Fleet in Hampstead, or the Effra River in Brixton, were enclosed in pipes: in less than half a century they had been transformed from country streams into tributaries of the main drainage system. London's water supply remained in private hands, however, until 1904.

The Metropolitan Board of Works not only laid out a new drainage system: it was also heavily involved in road widening and slum clearance. Soon it became clear that one of the consequences of its improvements was the destruction of yet more working-class housing of the cheapest sort, with no provision for its replacement. This further round of 'improvements', added to all the other road building schemes, railway and dock construction, and depopulation of the City

Free enterprise Victorian values led to disease and death in London during the first half of the nineteenth century, through Government failure to provide a decent sewage and water supply system. Top: Hideous slums on the banks of the Fleet Ditch, used as an open sewer, 1836. Centre: A poster of 1866 warns the people of Limehouse that the cholera epidemic was being spread by drinking unboiled water. Bottom: 'The Silent Highway-man – Your Money or Your Life', a Punch cartoon of 1858 satirizing the polluted Thames and the determination of the authorities to sacrifice human lives rather than spend public money on a sewage system

Construction of an outfall sewer and overflow into the River Lea, 1862. In the 1860s the Metropolitan Board of Works completed a new drainage and sewage system which fed into London's rivers, most of which were enclosed in pipes

to make way for warehouses and offices, aggravated terribly the problem of housing the poorest classes in London.

In the first half of the nineteenth century the evidence of government inquiries and the investigations of social reformers had demonstrated that in central London housing conditions were getting worse rather than better. The worsening sanitary condition of the capital also concentrated the poorest in foul tenements and lodging houses without a decent water supply or sewage system.

But it was not at all clear to the early Victorians who was to blame for this, and the dominant view seems to have been that the poor brought degradation on themselves. Much of the impulse for reform was based on the belief that what needed changing was the moral and spiritual welfare of slum-dwellers, though there were plenty of people who believed it was unreasonable to expect improvement if they lived in pigsties. The terrible spread of gin-drinking, crime, and the threat of social unrest, were all being connected with housing conditions before mid-century. Charles Dickens wrote in *Sketches by Boz*:

> Gin drinking is a great vice in England, but wretchedness and dirt are greater and until you improve the homes of the poor, or persuade a half-famished wretch not to seek relief in the temporary

oblivion of his own misery, with the pittance, which, divided among his family would furnish a morsel of bread for each, gin-shops will increase in number and splendour.

Lord Shaftesbury in 1851 made the connection between slum life and crime: 'Who would wonder that in these receptacles, nine-tenths of the great crimes, the burglaries, and murders and violence that desolated society were conceived and hatched?' And he, like Dickens, and other reformers, warned that whereas slums might breed revolution better housing could be of real importance to national security. 'The strength of the people rests upon the purity and firmness of the domestic system,' Lord Shaftesbury was quoted as saying in the 1860s. 'If the working man has his own house, I have no fear of revolution.'

But these arguments that social and political stability could be achieved through improved housing were in a sense ahead of their time, and neither Parliament nor the City of London were prepared to look at the problem in an efficient way. There were attempts from the mid-century onwards to force landlords to comply with new health regulations, but these neither tackled the roots of the problem, nor were they generally enforced. Housing, and the relief of poverty, was left to charity. This led to a range of responses, from the patronising moral and educational approach of such people as Octavia Hill, who in the 1860s attempted to teach household management to her tenants, to the frankly commercial philanthropy of the Metropolitan Association for Improving the Dwellings of the Industrious Classes.

At its first meeting in 1841, presided over by the Rector of Spitalfields, Henry Taylor, the Metropolitan Association included in its founding resolution: 'That an association be formed for the purpose of providing the labouring man with an increase of the comforts and conveniences of life, with full compensation to the capitalist.' In other words, the housing problem should be solved at a profit. This became the most popular solution, and was responsible in London – as elsewhere in the country – for the erection of large numbers of barrack-like tenement buildings, stark and cold to this day, but undoubtedly an immense improvement on the rookeries they replaced.

There were many other such commercially-minded charitable organizations, including the Society for Improving the Condition of the Labouring Classes, founded in 1844, which managed to win the admiration of Prince Albert so that their model dwellings were exhibited at the Great Exhibition in 1851. The whole movement became known as 'philanthropy at five per cent' though, compared with other investments, working-class housing was never a good bet and had difficulty attracting funds.

In a sense, the most successful of all philanthropic housing associations was that set up by the American millionaire George

Peabody, who came to England in 1837 and established himself as a merchant and banker. He donated £500,000 for a trust to be used solely to improve the conditions of the poor of London, regardless of religious or political sectarianism. The first trustees decided the best way to go about interpreting the aims of the trust was to build housing, which they did on a grand scale. Their efforts, which began with a formidable and rather ornate block in the Commercial Road in 1864, are still evident all over London, from the Wild Street estate in Covent Garden, to the massive development in Blackfriars.

Although the Peabody Trust was certainly charitable in its aims, and some commercial companies accused the trustees of under-charging on rents and under-cutting prices, the poorest of Londoners remained excluded. Despite the sparseness of the interiors of Peabody Buildings – the first blocks had no running water in the flats and no plaster on the walls – the rents were still too high for a large section of the population. In effect, Peabody was operating just like the 'philanthropy at five per

Peabody Square, Islington, the second Peabody estate, completed in 1865. Despite the paternalistic aims of George Peabody, the rents for flats in these barrack-like buildings were beyond the pocket of many working-class people

cent' housing associations, and until the 1880s it remained unthinkable that the homes of the poorest class of Londoners might in any way be provided for or subsidized by a public body not interested ultimately in profit.

An anonymous poem published in 1862 in the *City Press* expressed, apparently without irony, the mood of these endeavours:

Men of Money! shrewd and skill'd
In putting capital to nurse,
Ready to pull down streets, or build
If either helps to fill the purse, –
Now let me tell your wit a plan
How to reap a royal rent
Out of doing good to man –
Charity at cent per cent

But philanthropic housing did not make much of a profit. As the cost of central sites rose, so landowners such as the Duke of Bedford would sell off their slums to such companies and could ask a good price. It was very difficult to build to decent standards and at sufficient density to accommodate the same number of tenants – though not *the* same tenants – on the site of old housing that had been demolished. The people who moved in were very often lower middle class: clerks, policemen and 'respectable' artisans. The poorest classes were excluded on any significant scale, partly because they couldn't afford the rent, but also because they could not, or would not, conform to the rigid rules imposed by these associations, designed to make the poor respectable and to inculcate values of cleanliness, orderliness and thrift. Rules which specified no animals or 'home work' on the premises led to the exclusion of the underworld of Londoners who survived on messy and unsightly trades, like costers with their donkeys and refuse. These strict rules continued into this century and are clearly remembered by old tenants like Ellen Hill, who lived in the Peabody Dwellings in Stamford Street, Blackfriars, before the First World War.

The Shaftesbury Park Estate, built by the Artisans, Labourers and General Dwellings Company. This company differed from most other 'five per cent' philanthropic associations in that it built low-rise as opposed to high-rise housing estates

The stairs and the landing had to be polished until they were shining every week. All us children had to be vaccinated and you weren't allowed to play in the square outside after seven in the winter or after eight in the summer. And if you broke the rules or you didn't pay the rent each week, you were given a couple of hours to do it, to put your house in order, or you were out. Our superintendent was a real sergeant major type, a stickler for the rules, and we were a bit frightened of him, so most people did as they were told.

Charity, pure and simple, had by the 1880s become the principal means by which the wealthy in London tried to do something about the poverty which the great expansion of the metropolis had created. It existed on a fantastic scale, but was entirely disorganized, and so it was the central aim of a new organization, the Charity Organization Society, founded in 1869, to bring some order to this chaotic and inefficient form of social service. The C.O.S. believed that haphazard payments to the poor encouraged a 'scrounger' mentality and it introduced a kind of moral means test for applicants for charity, making relief dependent upon respectable behaviour. The C.O.S. and

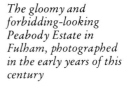

The gloomy and forbidding-looking Peabody Estate in Fulham, photographed in the early years of this century

the Poor Law Authorities were the forerunners of modern council-run social services. But in the 1880s the C.O.S. was chiefly concerned with ensuring that charity hand-outs were not squandered on poor people who did not repay philanthropy with cleanliness or godliness.

It was at this time that a really influential pamphlet was published which began a shift in national attitudes towards the problems of

A page from the tenants record book of the Peabody Dwellings in Stamford Street, Blackfriars. The book shows that a number of tenants were evicted for non-payment of rent or disorderly conduct – evidence of the determination of philanthropic housing organizations to discipline morally their tenants

metropolitan poverty. In 1883, *The Bitter Cry of Outcast London* – published anonymously, but generally attributed to the Rev. Andrew Mearns – once again laid bare the horrors of working-class housing. According to *Reynold's Newspaper*, 'The revelations concerning "Outcast London" cause a tremendous sensation and thrill of horror throughout the land.'

per Week.

DATE OF LEAVING.	REMARKS.
10 March /84	Removed to No. 7 L
24 March 1884	Received Notice for Disorderly Conduct
8 Sept 1884	Gave Notice
7 May 1888	Removed to Pimlico
14 Sept 1891	Gave Notice
8 Augt 1892	Removed to No. 2 J
13 July 1896	Removed to No. 17 K
died	? date

NOTICE.

The attention of Tenants is called to Rule 4, which must be strictly complied with. The Passages and Steps must be swept every morning before 10 o'clock. The Sink, Closet and Laundry Windows must be cleaned every Friday or Saturday. This must be done by the Tenants in turn.

BY ORDER.

NOTICE.

It having been brought to the notice of the Trustees that some tenants are taking in washing—

Rule 5 must be STRICTLY ENFORCED. Any tenant infringing this will receive NOTICE TO QUIT.

BY ORDER.

The strict, regimental style of the Peabody Trust is captured by these notices which were pinned up at the turn of the century. One effect of the insistence on cleanliness and respectable behaviour was to exclude a large section of the poorest classes. The banning of home-based work, such as taking in washing, kept out families dependent on such trades

The first impulse of those affected by this, and a whole spate of newspaper reports, was to step up charitable activity. It became common for fashionable ladies to go 'slumming' in the East End, which was held up as the region suffering the worst poverty, though many other districts of London were in as miserable a condition. After the 1886 riots, described at the beginning of this chapter, the flow of charity turned into a torrent. A fund had been launched for the unemployed by the Lord Mayor of London, and on 8 February – the day of the riot – stood at £3,300. By 23 February it had reached £60,000, and finally totalled £78,000.

The Charity Organization Society, which detested this kind of un-thought-out, emotional giving, was severely critical of the fund. Finally Parliament too began to realize that dependence on this kind of spontaneous and disorganized solution to the immense problems of housing and poverty was unsatisfactory. London did need some form of local government which could begin to relieve the misery of a large, and increasingly threatening, section of the population. The old *laissez-faire* doctrine, that private enterprise could best find a solution, was beginning to crumble, and the connection between housing and poverty became not just the theory of social reformers but the received wisdom.

Although the argument that London's government should be reformed once and for all was gradually accepted, there was a protracted argument about whether it would be best served by a single authority, or by a number of new local authorities which took into account the new districts Victorian expansion had created. The powerful West End vestries opposed 'centralism' – the East End vestries supported it. In the end the 'centralists' won, and in 1888 the London County Council was founded. Throughout the 1880s, when radical liberal groups were pressing for a single London authority, they wanted control of the police. But the Home Office fiercely opposed this, and won.

The first elections were held in 1889, and the L.C.C. took over the area and functions of the Metropolitan Board of Works. It was an authority split between radical and liberal groups, and in the first few years lacked any effective powers. But London had almost for the first time been recognized for what it was: a single metropolis, the largest the world had ever seen. The first most pressing task of the new authority was to tackle the housing problem which, by the end of the century, it was beginning to do in a much more extensive way than had ever been possible before. After the Housing of the Working Classes Act of 1890, enabling public authorities to build housing themselves, the L.C.C. began its building programme with the Boundary Street estate in Bethnal Green, which replaced a notorious slum, the Jago.

But the fear of a powerful London authority able to challenge the

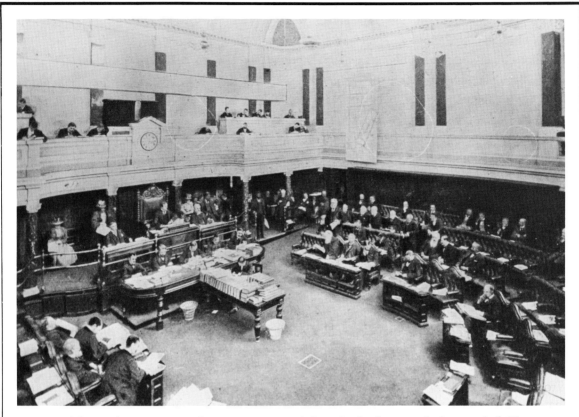

A sitting of the London County Council in the 1900s. Founded in 1888, two years after the riots, it began to tackle the immense problems of need for housing and transport, of poverty, and of organizational chaos, which laissez-faire Victorian values had helped to create

power of Westminster and the City had not entirely receded. Ten years after the creation of the L.C.C., the first London boroughs were set up, partly with the intention of undermining the new metropolitan county's position.

London went into the twentieth century with a brand new administrative structure finally recognizing its massive existence – though the L.C.C. boundaries were already well inside the true frontiers of the metropolis, which was still expanding at a considerable rate. The City, by now with a population of only twenty-seven thousand out of a total of well over five million Londoners, remained proudly aloof, as it does today.

London did not change overnight with all these new developments, but it had entered a new phase in its history. In the fields of social policy and local government, the foundations had been laid for the enormous expansion of the built-up area of London in the 1920s and 30s, when the L.C.C. engaged on a massive housing programme, building new suburbs along the electric Tube and tram lines, while the centre of town became rapidly depopulated. Moreover, the population of the metropolis was no longer rising by leaps and bounds, so that the new housing that was built privately and by local authorities created suburbia for a much larger number of Londoners.

We have taken the first years of the nineteenth century as the point when 'modern' London began to merge with the great expansion of population, the building of wave upon wave of new suburbs, and the great division of the metropolis into its East and West Ends. These terms are still used today, but with a rather different meaning. And the historical period when the social and political atmosphere of London began to change – when, in a sense, the West rediscovered the East – was in the 1880s, precisely the period when there were riots, such as those of 1886, which in moments of panic brought the social poles together and created fear.

For it was in the 1880s and 90s that the modern ideas of the West End as a less exclusive area, and of the East End as a kind of jolly musical-hall place, full of chirpy Cockneys, started to form. The threat of 'outcast' London was lifting, and with it the fear of the dangerous classes.

In inner London, the old fears, suspicions and antagonisms of the nineteenth century gave way, as the centre was rapidly abandoned, to new social frontiers, new problems and new antagonisms, which are really the story of the metropolis in the inter-war period. But that is another story, which we hope to tackle in another television series and another book. The nineteenth-century legacy, however, has never altogether disappeared in London, and remains as an intriguing and, in many places, an observable record of the capital of the Empire when it was the largest and wealthiest city in the world.

Further Reading

Out of the many books that we have read, the following were particularly interesting and informative. For a general overview of London in the nineteenth century, Francis Sheppard's *London 1808-1870 The Infernal Wen* (Secker & Warburg 1971) is far and away the best on the subject. H.J. Dyos and M. Wolff (eds), *The Victorian City*, 2 vols, (Routledge & Kegan Paul 1973) has several useful essays on London history. A period 'feel' of life in London can be found in Henry Mayhew, *London Labour and the London Poor* (1861) and George Sims (ed), *Living London* (Cassell 1906)

Although no books have been written which directly link the expansion of City institutions with the growth and character of London, W. Rubinstein, *Men of Property* (Croom Helm 1981) contains a good account of the staggering wealth of the City in the nineteenth century. For the life-style of clerks, see Geoff Crossick (ed), *The Lower Middle Class* (Croom Helm 1973), which is social in its approach, H.G. de Fraine, *Servant of This House: Life in the Old Bank of England* (Constable 1960), which is autobiography, and the famous diary of the fictional Pooter, G. and W. Grossmith, *Diary of a Nobody* (Dent 1977-reprint of 1892 edition). On the West End there are relevant sections in Leonore Davidoff, *The Best Circles: Society, Etiquette and The Season* (Croom Helm 1973), Alison Adburgham, *Shops and Shopping 1800-1914* (Allen & Unwin 1981), *The Survey of London*, Vol. 39, (1977), and Patricia Malcolmson, 'Getting a Living in the Slums of Victorian Kensington' in *The London Journal*, 1977. On the East End, see Peter Hall, *The Industries of London since 1861* (Hutchinson 1962), Gareth Stedman Jones, *Outcast London* (Clarendon 1971), Jerry White, *Rothschild Buildings: Life in an East End Tenement Block 1887-1920* (Routledge & Kegan Paul 1980), Bill Fishman, *The Streets of East London* (Duckworth 1979), Arthur Bryant, *Liquid History* (Port of London Authority 1960). On transport, see T. Barker and M. Robbins, *A History of London Transport Vol. 1: The Nineteenth Century* (Allen & Unwin 1975), John Kellett, *The Impact of Railways in Victorian Cities* (Routledge & Kegan Paul 1969), and David Reeder, 'A Theatre of Suburbs: Some patterns of Development in West London, 1801-1911' in H.J. Dyos (ed), *The Study of Urban History* (Edward Arnold 1968).

We found the best books on the development of the suburbs to be F.M.L. Thompson, *Hampstead, Building a Borough 1650-1964* (Routledge & Kegan Paul 1974), M. Hunter, *The Victorian Villas of Hackney* (Hackney Society 1981), D. Olsen, *The Growth of Victorian London* (Peregrine Books 1979) and H.J. Dyos, *Victorian Suburb: A Study of the Growth of Camberwell* (1961). You can find out what sort of people lived in a particular area from the social maps in the many volumes of Charles Booth's *Life and Labour of the People in London* (Macmillan 1902).

On radical politics, the mob, charity and reform, see David Goodway, *London Chartism 1838-1848* (Cambridge University Press 1982), A. Wohl, *The Eternal Slum: Housing and Social Policy in Victorian London* (Edward Arnold 1977), Henry Jephson, *The Sanitary Evolution of London* (1907), G.S. Jones, *Outcast London* (see above), and Ken Young and Patricia Garside, *Metropolitan London* (Edward Arnold 1982).

Index

Page numbers in italic indicate illustrations.

INDEX